WALK WITH D.I.G.N.I.T.Y.

DOING IN GOD'S NAME

INCREDIBLE THINGS YOURSELF

MACY V. BUTLER

Published by:
Antwon Publishing Company Inc.
Winter Haven, Florida 33881
863-307-7408

ISBN: 978-0-9882792-1-6
ISBN: 978-0-9882792-2-3

Author/Publisher: Macy V. Butler
Edited By: Gloria Howell, Rogers, Arkansas
Book Design and Layout by: Antwon Publishing
Company Inc. and Kenneth Monts, KJB Graphic
Designs & Marketing Consulting / Promotions
Houston, TX / Little Rock, AR
Ph. 281-730-1854
Printed in the United States of America

This book is a work of nonfiction; the names of
people and places mentioned are actual and true.

Dedication Page

To my dearest and beloved wife, Gwendolyn who always had faith in me, I will always love you. And I hope this book will provides us some rewards and comfort for the rest of our lives

My Love

This book is also dedicated to the memory of someone I met one day who became a mentor and friend, Dick Gregory.

Table of Contents

The organization D.I.G.N.I.T.Y. humble beginnings came from an inspiration in a speech one man received on Easter morning in 1991 from another man about men's responsibility to his community and family.

Doing In God's Name Incredible Things Yourself acronym was created by Bernard Murray, a Muslim member of Masjid Ameen Zakariya after hearing the speech and talking to State Representative Bill Walker Jr., a Baptist Christian.

Through this collaborative effort an organization was spiritually ordained to encourage black men throughout the city to become part of something special that would help change the face and direction of Little Rock, Arkansas forever.

Comedian and famed civil rights leader Dick Gregory heard what the organization D.I.G.N.I.T.Y. was doing to combat the scourge of drug abuse and gang violence. While traveling through Little Rock he joined the cause and was warmly accepted, arrested and helped transform the organization into a mechanism that allowed its message of hope to be shared through many public forums.

This story is a journey of faith and determination of some dedicated special men who came together because of their love for their neighborhoods and city. Love is the most common denominator that allowed for the organization's immediate success and miraculous progress that was accomplished in a short period.

Even though it seemed forever as we walked those dangerous streets each and every night for over two years. This is my recollection of those events.

Chapter One
Another Funeral

What is happening to me? I was becoming numb to it. Here I am attending the forty third funeral in the past four years of a young black male who has died from violence on the streets of Little Rock, Arkansas. This time it is the youngest son of Vernon and Dorothy

Patten, friends of mine since the early 70's.

He was just one of many young black males and females (but primarily males) whose lives were snuffed out because of this epidemic black-on-black shootings and killings associated with the street gangs who now littered my beloved streets of Little Rock.

In 1979 I moved to northwest Arkansas to begin a brief three year career as Arkansas' first black wildlife officer in Benton County. When I moved to Benton County with my wife and son we were the only black family living in the entire county. When I was fired as a wildlife officer in 1982 I continued living up there because we really loved living in Bella Vista, Arkansas. I quickly found another good paying job working for Wal-Mart executive Charlie Needham as the head chef of his new exclusive restaurant and club, Charlie's Place. I loved the tranquil rustic lifestyle but I really stayed as an act of defiance to the crooked Sheriff Don Rystrom, the man who cost me my career as a wildlife officer. When he was arrested for being a crooked sheriff I was determined not to leave Benton County until his trial and criminal conviction. I would leave on my terms but you will have to read my first book, "Where Did the Cotton Go?" for that story.

4

Now the father of two boys, one a twelve year old, I knew puberty was soon going to require that for my son's safety I needed to get them back into an environment that would be easier to assimilate and less dangerous.

As a child Lamont, my oldest, never felt racism from the people we associated with. But now ready to enter middle school and being the only black child in the school was something I was not going to risk. We moved back to Little Rock in 1986.

With my background in the juvenile justice field I quickly landed a good paying job working for the Division of

Children & Families at Alexander Youth Services Center Intensive Treatment Unit.

There were a lot of familiar faces there. People I knew in the profession during the mid 70's so being a state employee again was a fairly smooth transition for me.

The Intensive Treatment Unit is where the boys who are sentenced for major crimes such as murder, rape, robbery and serious deviant behavior issues are housed. A lot of these kids continue on with these behaviors into the adult prison systems. I quickly began learning about the gangs and their influence in the juvenile community. I learned the various names of the many gang sets around the state, their gang recruitment techniques and gang behaviors because we were always confiscating gang paraphernalia, writing the students up for throwing and teaching gang-signs to the new recruits who generally were the kids sentenced to the unit from the rural Arkansas communities.

I created what I referred to as "my gang bible" a thick collection of the many rules and signs of the different sets, the tattoos and graffiti and even how their clothing is worn to give signals to each other. Each recruit was required to record, memorize and then destroy all gang knowledge but during searches I kept the confiscated materials. I documented the knowledge mainly for self preservation but the information I gathered would help deter a lot of attacks on potential victims. It also gave me props with the gangs and help keep down incidents on my shift.

I found Alexander and Pine Bluff Youth Services Centers to be the youth gangs teaching academies where they taught each other criminal behavior. How to replicate the gang mentality so when they returned to their communities they continued the education of their peers.

All the state- funded systems could do was provide care and custody. A lot of their behaviors we are not equipped to handle except for daily crisis interventions.

As a state employee with benefits I was basically guaranteed a stable salary with annual step increases plus benefits for my family along with a two-week annual vacation that we usually spent in Florida. This is a career where you can go through the motions and function for many years but never really make a difference in the lives of the clients we service. I did my job but after about six years and continuing to see the same kids regularly returning and basically watching them grow up in the system, I began to feel useless and burned out as a service provider.

It was one kid, Gary Dailey that really affected me and changed my whole focus.

I first met Gary when he came to us at the tender age of twelve.

Gary was convicted of forcible rape and sodomy which meant he would be with us for a few years. He was a very likable little guy from a small town who very quickly adapted to the correctional system. Violent sex crime offenders live in single, no-roommate rooms and Gary kept his hygiene and house impeccable.

It was his knowledge of the gangs that made him very popular to the other boys looking for that information.

But Gary is also a psychopath and sexual sadist. Being somewhat tall for his young age, he left the impression that he might be older than he looked. Gary spent two Christmas' with us before they let him out in the spring but he was back for his third Christmas that same year. Working with Gary on a daily basis meant I had a lot of interactive time with him. He quickly learned how to approach staff. He knew which buttons to push to create hostile situations among the other students and if pushed himself would react violently and quickly but never towards staff. He made great efforts to keep staff on his good side which helped mediate a lot of the incidents he was involved in.

The state did not provide a barber service for the student's hygiene housed at Alexander so many of them had long unkempt and uncut hair.

I decided to invest in a barber kit and received permission from my supervisor to begin cutting the boys hair on the unit. I thought if we provided this minor humanity service I could use it as a mentoring tool to help them raise their self-esteem, change behaviors and at least feel good about themselves. I also used it as a way to show them I did care about them and tried to tell them of other options once they left and returned home. It was also a reward for good behavior on the unit.

Gary was vain about his appearance so he spent a lot of time grooming and always wanted me to trim him up or new style high-low cut to the point I thought this kid might even be worth the effort. He was intelligent, well spoken and could be very well-mannered when he wanted to.

Alexander released Gary for the final time just after his sixteenth birthday.

Before Gary would turn seventeen he would be charged as an adult for a double-homicide and sentenced to life in prison because of his extensive juvenile criminal record.

When Gary and so many other kids that I knew personally kept getting rearrested I began to lose hope with the state correctional system realizing we really were not helping these kids.

I decided then that if I am going to continue to work in this field and with young people to make a difference I would have to concentrate on reaching those kids before they got into the system. Some are calling them the "Lost Generation" because of the influences of gangs, drugs, sexy videos, and violent video games.

Here I am standing before the casket of a child I knew about before his birth. I saw no end to the continuing escalation of violence and death on the streets of Little Rock and it made me truly fearful for my three sons. It now was becoming all too common to hear loud gunshot blasts close by in the neighborhood from many different kinds of weapons to the point you could almost identify what weapon was being fired just by the way it sounded.

So sad.

It is now March 1991 and violent street crime particularly involving juveniles is even more astounding with major street crime up by eleven percent compared to the same period in 1990.

Homicides and aggravated assault statistics are approaching thirty percent. One third of the suspects arrested for murder in Little Rock in 1990 were teenagers. Now father to three boys I truly worried about my eldest now seventeen, becoming more under the influence of peer pressure, plus the lure of quick easy money from selling illicit drugs, the appeal from hip-hop gansta rap music that he too may be affected and fall prey to this growing scourge.

Little Rock is no different from any other urban city. In the past ten years many cities around the country saw the growing infiltration of Chicago and west coast gangs particularly the Crips and the Bloods.

These criminal violent enterprises were becoming the new family for thousands of disenfranchised and some time fatherless black males. They are now being recruited with the lure of family unity, easy money and flashy material things that many young black and Latino males became willing participants to sell drugs mainly crack cocaine, heroin and marijuana.

The Crips & Bloods violent presence in our neighborhoods was a signal they intended to maintain control of these lucrative criminal enterprises in our neighborhoods with many exotic weapons such as AK-47's, 9 mm Glocks, M-16 Assault rifles and shotguns all with the ability to deliver many rounds are used to commit indiscriminate drive-by shootings at times resulting in brutal death. The two basic colors of blue and red would draw deadly indiscriminate violent reactions just from the mere wearing of the apparel.

Now as I stood by numb, looking at this dead child whom I knew before he knew himself and watching his grieving parents, I was determined that if something is to be done, I would have to be willing to do more than just stand by.

Little Rock is rich in civil rights history of advocacy and strength starting with Central High School, Daisy Bates and the Little Rock Nine. I grew up during those times knowing most of these people, strong people within their own abilities.

I became angry.

Angry at myself for giving in to these street thugs who possessed no titles of property ownership, paid no taxes or made no investment to claim and take control over the very same streets I too grew up on and still loved. I took the attitude if it is to be, then why not me. I knew I had to do something. I just didn't know what or how or when.

So I prayed about it.

Chapter Two
Answered Prayers

It is March the sixteenth my birthday. I am thirty-eight years old. To reward myself I decided to buy myself a few new personal items so I stopped by Jamal's Import on Wright Avenue & High Street. Khatib Jamal Safee-ullah is a local businessman and Muslim. He owned a hat and apparel store. I only recently began shopping at his place. I found it a few months earlier while taking a short-cut through the old Professional Building parking lot off of Wright Avenue.

I noticed the small clothing store there and decided to return to see what he sold. Jamal sold items like Bob Marly t-shirts, nice caps, sunglasses, jewelry, body oils and other things that appealed to the young adult and at a reasonable price.

As a child growing up near Wright Avenue & High Street a major intersection about two blocks from where Daisy Bates still lives the Professional building was an important location for the community back then because it housed the offices of our prominent black physicians, a pharmacy and provided other social services in the community at a major intersection in the black community.

 But now through growth of the city the relocation of the black middle class into other parts of Little Rock the neighborhood was in fast decline from lack of attention.

This intersection soon became prime territory for the gangs because of the cheap large houses in close proximity, a few small anchor businesses still holding on and the nearby schools still drew large populations of people and allowed the ability to navigate without much notice. I lived here, I grew up here, and I went to school here. I graduated college here. So my history is here, the dynamics and the infrastructure of this neighborhood are an integral part of my being.

It was during this birthday self-indulgence while shopping I got into a discussion with an old childhood friend and now a Muslim Emanuel Muhammad. He too grew up here and we have known each other for many years. He and I began talking about how the neighborhood is changing. The violence at our old hangout, the carwash, with the gangs is now daily occurrences with drive-by shootings. There were several other men there at Jamal's from the local mosque. They also talked about some of the crazy antics we ourselves did as youth while growing up but that things are now spiraling downward getting worse.

We were basically relinquishing our neighborhood to the gangs who are in reality our own children. I did not know any of these guys personally but I felt an immediate kinship with what we were talking about. One of them mentioned others were talking about the same thing and that they were planning a meeting in the coming days to devise an action plan and that I was welcome to attend.

I was intrigued but I did not have a lot of knowledge of the Muslim community other than a few friends I knew growing up who converted and we still maintain friendships like I had with Emanuel.

The Masjid converted from a nightclub formerly known as the Cavalier's Club. My father frequented it a lot. I really learned about the Cavalier's Club at age fifteen. I found out that trying to sneak into certain clubs will get you in big trouble especially if you get caught by your daddy. I made only one visit into the Cavalier's Club as a teenager but it would be a lifelong memory.

I was hanging out with some older friends one night when they decided to see if we could sneak into the club. The famed blues artist Albert King was performing a concert.

This would mean a lot of different faces would be coming into the club making it easier for us to slip in. The man who ran the club is a good friend of my father and he knew me but had not seen me in a while. Back in those days they did not check for identification. I wasn't there ten minutes before I got spotted by my daddy and when we made eye contact I

immediately shrunk to the size of a grape
and made a hasty roll up out of there.
He did not follow me nor did he ever say
a word to me that night but I did hear
later he let the guy running the nightclub
have it for letting me in. I never went
back into the Cavalier's Club even after
my father died of a heart attack later or
even after I turned twenty-one.

Arkansas State Representative William
"Bill" Walker Jr. spoke at the Masjid
during the Easter holiday observance.
His speech was about empowerment and
reclamation. He urged those there to
become more proactive and concerned
for their community and their children.

He talked about the gangs, drugs and the perpetual violence in the neighborhoods.

There was one man there who really took what Bill had to say to heart and he challenged and vigorously implored his fellow Muslims to act accordingly.

They prayed about it.

It is now the first week in April of 1991 and still intrigued I decided to again stop by Jamal's and see what they were thinking about doing. Jamal told me that they had already held brainstorming sessions and that another one would be held the next day. He invited me to attend. When I arrived the next day there were already several cars parked in the parking lot and in front of Jamal's store.

As I walked up there were a couple of men also about to enter and they greeted me, "Assalaamu 'alaykum".
WA `alaykumu salaam I responded back to them.

Upon entering the store a salesperson directed us to another part of the store that appeared to be a storage room for inventory and a small office. There were four other men already there to greet us.

I met Yusuf Ali, Johnny Hasan, Bernard Murray, Muhammad Rasheed and Jamal was there too. He stated that the meeting would be starting soon they were just waiting on a few more people they knew were coming to arrive. A few minutes later in walked two other men.

They are Bill Walker Jr. and Rev. Ricky Hicks.

After handshakes and some exchanges of names we began talking about why we were here and how we would organize, and develop a strategy to reclaim Wright Avenue. We were not vigilantes nor did we want to be confrontational to create more violence. It was decided that we would start on Wright Avenue since it was most visible and in the middle of the city's highest crime zone. It was a major drug trafficking area and a prominent street that everyone knew and it was close to the Masjid for added security.

Other than Jamal and Emanuel who had now arrived the only other person there I am familiar with is Bill Walker.

Bill and I are not friends but I knew his whole family. His sister Cheryl and I were friends. We once went to the same junior high school though she was two grades behind me. She had a friend that had a crush on me and I would meet up with her a lot at Cheryl's house.

His older brother Jimmy played football at famed Little Rock Central High School Tigers, later played for the Arkansas

Razorbacks football team in Fayetteville and a few years as a professional. I think Bill was the third of four siblings and much younger than me so I did not know him growing up other than as a little boy.

Later as a young adult he ran locally for political office winning a seat on the county directors. He then went on to campaign successfully for the state legislature and was now serving as a state representative. As a young man he was gaining a reputation in the political arena as someone who represented the black community in state government and was becoming an influential voice and public person in Little Rock.

But it was the Reverend Rickey Hicks who stood out from the norm. Ricky, a local attorney, pastor of a church and also operated his own physical therapy business.

Rickey now resides in Little Rock but did not grow up there nor did he live in any of the areas of concern. He's a successful businessman living in the suburbs basically far removed from Little Rock's daily violence.

The AME church he pastor's however is located on Main Street heading into the south end of Little Rock where there is heavy gang activity and a poorer section of Little Rock. I also surmised that through his law practice he encountered many seeking legal advice from criminal arrests and personal injury accidents. At first I thought he was there with Bill to give us legal advice to help the group legally form the organization.

Rickey is the real deal.

The meeting began with a prayer by Imam Johnny Hasan. Johnny is one of the religious leaders at the Masjid. Johnny Hasan is a confident man I guessed to be in his early forties and is about five feet six but he spoke with clarity, knowledge and purpose.

Bernard Murray is the same age as me and is somewhat more analytical and speaks as an educated man. It was actually Bernard who penned the name for the group which succinctly identified who and what we are about.

DIGNITY.

The name DIGNITY which is the acronym for Doing in God's Name Incredible Things Yourself.

When I first heard the name and its meaning I felt a personal sense of ownership, independence and direction within this dynamic group collective. DIGNITY means the quality of being worthy of esteem, honor and of high repute.

God answering prayers is a part of everything we would do.

Bernard stated that he and others at the Masjid had unsuccessfully attempted to curtail the drug trafficking on Wright Avenue by talking to the residents but then Bill spoke to them of successful efforts in other communities to thwart crime. It was the inspiration from that speech that motivated the Muslim group to organize more sincerely.

There was also an immediate spiritual connection we shared that showed our love for our God.

We also recognized that when we went out into the community we wanted to appear as a unified but dignified group of men which also meant taking on some characteristics and behaviors that nearly every organizing entity including the gangs do and that is to look alike but unique.

We too wanted to be clearly identifiable when we worked as a unit.

Bill and some of the others went down to Bennett's Military Supply store on Main Street to select the clothing that would serve our purpose. They bought items and presented to us a structured official look with black paratroop type jumpsuits with webbed belts, or denim cargo pants. A t-shirt was created with the DIGNITY words and a red clenched fist emblem that showed strength, combat boots, and black caps that also had the name of the organization embroidered in red with a green star symbolizing freedom and justice.

When they modeled the uniform for us we all agreed that it was just the look we wanted to portray and was appropriate for our needs.

We worked on a few chants such as "Who are we?" "DIGNITY", "Up with hope, down with dope" so that when we walked down the streets or stood in front of the dope houses that it would be clear of our intent and what we represented.

We also equipped ourselves with a few prevention items such as hand held walkie-talkies, a bullhorn, black long handled flashlights and a video camera to record our activities.

We practiced how we would march into the neighborhood as a group, and how we approached the people initially and that we would never separate from each other as a unit. We also decided as an organization we would have a chain of cooperation to maintain cohesiveness and order. We transformed ourselves from ordinary men of color and faith in God into men of determination striving to achieve extraordinary things in a community that we all loved so much.

Jamal, Bernard, Bill and Rickey are recognized as the co-founders, Jamal is viewed as president, Bill vice-president, Johnny spiritual leader, and Rickey treasury and legal.

I must admit that we truly functioned as an unusually unique coalition of talented men all believing that the people in the community have some responsibility to solve some of its own problems. We had questions but we also had some remedies.

Understanding the extreme danger and ultimate sacrifice going into something like this made each of us reflect on our intent and the decision was made to continue. We made a conscious decision not to give notice to immediate local law enforcement of our plans nor ask for permission or any assistance.

We also understood that this is not something we're going to just start for a

few days and then stop. We were
determined to continue until we made a
definite impact and brought real attention
to our cause.

The meeting ended in prayer.

We are now ready to begin our mission
of hope and reclamation.

We decided to begin the daily marches
immediately that same week on April
Fool's Day.

A few days after Easter we met back at
Jamal's just before dark. We assembled
in the parking lot. Everyone on this night
wore the black jumpsuits and I must
admit that I was awed by the way we
looked.

We looked good, professional but most importantly we were still dignified. For this inaugural march there were approximately fifteen men who came out.

Some were lower-profile personalities representing a mixture of religious, occupations and motivations. More than half were Muslim but the group also included Baptist, African Methodist Episcopalians and members of other Christian non-denominations.

Some members were reformed drug abusers, while others had never used drugs.

Some had prison records while another was an Arkansas State Police trooper.

Many of us held college degrees, were married with children and maintained stable lifestyles.

We never went on patrol without first prayer for the safety and understanding of everyone including those we encountered.

Standing two abreast we formed a line to embark on a historic journey that none could have foreseen as the beginning of something truly remarkable but not necessarily unique for Little Rock. I must admit I was nervous about what we were about to do because the gangs were dangerous, violent, and not fearful of anyone and for too-long had used strong-arm tactics and deadly force to achieve their goals.

But we would operate on the principal to instill the can-do spirit, reclaim privilege and responsibility to prove to the world that despite what it thinks, we got what it takes with the hope no one gets attacked or injured.

Chapter Three
Up With Hope, Down With Dope

We began our first patrol proceeding west up Wright Avenue in earnest and in full cadence.

The gauntlet now being truly thrown we began the chants, "Up with hope, down with dope", "Who are we?" Dignity! I can only imagine what we must have looked like to the bewildered people who drove past us as we shouted out our proclamations of hope.

People blew their car horns, some shouted obscenities, some waved in support of our efforts while others stood in awe seeing a dozen black men in military dress walking along Wright Avenue using bullhorns and flash lights to gain attention all the while videotaping what is happening.

At the intersection of Wright Avenue and High Street is our designated first stop, the carwash. The carwash is the prime hangout for young people with shiny cars, girls, drugs and money. That carwash was built not long after I got my first car back in 1970.

It was one of the main locations you went to clean your ride, meet up with friends and chase girls. Back then you would see at any given time ten to fifteen cars, but now it is jammed packed with almost a hundred cars and even more kids driving around in and out all night long. It was a popular spot for years plus being centrally located, Wright Avenue was one of the main traffic arteries heading east west north and south in Little Rock. High Street basically went from the state capitol to the south end section of town which is majority black.

Thousands of vehicles went through that intersection daily.

Back then it was a fun place. Now it is deadly territory as the crossover traffic route of the main rival gangs that now permeate the city. Young people congregated there by the hundreds daily with many instances of criminal behavior, assaults, drug activity from the crack cocaine market and vice crimes being reported and targeted regularly by the police.

The carwash is the first test to see how we will survive this night and because it is the closest stop location on our first patrol.

As we walked up to the carwash our chants were already in progress.

"Up with hope, down with dope".

"Who are we?"

"DIGNITY"!

We were now men bonded and united armed with our faith in God we approached the crowds confidently and boldly.

Without any previous planning we formed a single file extending around the corner of the carwash on Wright Avenue and High with flashlights beaming and video cameras rolling.

The way we were dressed and I guess seeing we were older black men but somewhat familiar, none of the people at the carwash approached us with disrespect and just watched us with curiosity.

Some of them were startled by the scene reacted defensively and began shouting non-directed profanity. But we stood our ground continuing our chants.

As some chanted, Jamal, Bill, Johnny and I are familiar faces to a lot of them so we initiated the first contact with some of the young people we knew. I grew up in two different houses in the neighborhood first on Fourteenth & Ringo St and later on Twenty-first and Battery Street.

Just a block away is Arkansas Baptist College where I graduated, so I am no stranger to this neighborhood.

During the earlier years when I was away from Little Rock in northwest Arkansas, the neighborhood had gradually deteriorated due to the flight of the middle-class blacks to west Little Rock.

God was with us tonight because as we stood our ground the cars began to leave with their music blaring and the low-rider cars screeching their tires.

Other cars quickly replaced those that left the parking spaces but they too were checking us out.

That night was basically a peaceful stand-off and after about an hour in front of the carwash we moved the patrol on up Wright Avenue towards Battery Street about four blocks away where there was another popular carwash and store. Along the way on both sides of the street there were many other small black businesses.

There was Dubission Funeral Home, of course two liquor stores, Smitty's night club, Say McIntosh Barbecue, Brashwell Barbecue, Wood's Pool Hall, Mathis Cleaners, the Vegetable Market, the Masjid, a shine parlor, Charles's Minute Mart and Allean's House of Beauty.

There were more businesses to the west but our primary target was five blocks up to Battery Street where the most violence and crime was occurring daily.

The houses in the area were large stately two story middle-class homes of some of Little Rock's most prominent black people during the fifties, sixties and seventies.

There were two historical black liberal arts colleges within four blocks of each other.

Now the black primary financial infrastructure is displaced and the neighborhood lay prey and abandoned. Blocks were claimed and infiltrated by the many gangs that took over various sections of Little Rock while city leaders lived in denial thinking gangs were a west coast-east coast problem.

We walked approximately six blocks along one side of the street, occasionally stopping to interact with anyone we felt we should talk to.

We targeted those we identified as boozers, prostitutes, gamblers, drug dealers or anyone acting suspicious. We would encourage them to move on and that this type of anti-social behavior is no longer being condoned.

If we saw anything that looked like a crime we would contact the police. We put out notice warning that this area is now being declared drug and crime free.

Of course there was immediate resistance by those we targeted and we were cursed and threatened but we were not deterred from our mission. We felt somewhat secure in our numbers and the equipment we had on hand to document any criminal activity noticed.

For the most part the people taken off guard just moved on.

Some were curious and approached to get more information about the group, what we were doing and what we hoped to accomplish.

Many were supportive just to see someone now taking a stand of vigilance in the neighborhood. This was an area that had seen multiple shootings, killings, rapes, and drug dealing over the past year.

Last November a man had been shot in a narcotics dispute at Wright Avenue & Wolfe Street. Robert Haney, 78, was killed in a March gambling incident at 1720 W. 16th St.

There were several abandoned houses where an array of discarded liquor bottles that revealed its main function as a hangout for drinking, gambling and drug dealing. We quickly found out in our attempt to take our neighborhood back that most criminals are really cowards.

Like roaches, once you turn the lights on they flee.

That night the only resistance we encountered was from the drug dealers whose business activity we interrupted when we would point the video cameras either at them and their potential customers looking for drugs, as we shouted our chants, "up with hope down with dope."

I don't know if it was the enthusiasm that we felt from seeing what we were actually accomplishing or the adrenaline, but we would not leave the patrol that night until about four in the morning.

We returned back to Jamal's store to get our vehicles and head home to rest up, go to our day jobs and prepare for the next night of patrol.

When I got home I shared what happened with Gwen my wife who was extremely nervous and concerned about me going out in the first place. But I shared with her how successful the patrol was and the different encounters we ensued.

She was fearful of us being individually targeted in retaliation but she knew of my determination that whenever I made my mind up to do something that I would follow through and do what I felt was right. She followed me all of the way to Rogers, Arkansas when I became the first black to work in the state of Arkansas as a Wildlife Officer. Again putting her life and my life at risk for the chance to do something unique and special with my life.

I also warned her that with God's protection I was there for the long haul.

That next evening after a full day of work and short nap I got dressed and returned for another night of patrolling with the men of DIGNITY.

When I arrived most of the guys were already there assessing the events from the previous night and how the patrol went. We all agreed that the impact of our actions would definitely soon generate some response from the local businesses and the people who live in the area.

There was now a buzz on the streets that these crazy guys were marching and that there may be some retaliation from those we were trying to displace.

The one thing that helped us be more effective particularly early on, was that the only people aware of what we were doing was within the Black Muslim community. Many of the locals did not know or see this as a collective joint effort of black men who cared for their community. So the patrols that Saturday and for the next week were somewhat a low key adventure. But we continued to meet light resistance from those who didn't want us there. A few made verbal threats but nothing overtly or personal.

With safety in numbers with our equipment plus being on a street with a constant flow of traffic gave us visibility. We began to gain some notoriety and obvious support from the people who knew what we represented.

It gave us a sense of accomplishment and pride. As each day passed more and more people gained knowledge of us. Some good some bad but at least they were talking about it.

After about a week we decided to get another place to meet to avoid any possible retaliation from Jamal and his business in case he is targeted. Within the Professional Building complex in another building across from Jamal's we

rented a small room to meet and store
our equipment. We also decided to park
our vehicles at different locations close
by so that until we had a better grasp of
the situation no individual would be
singled out for attack.

It took about a week before the local
news papers found out about us
patrolling on Wright Avenue.

Of course with Bill being a state
representative and known in the city,
Rickey a young upcoming attorney and
minister, it did not take long before a
reporter showed up wanting to do a story
on the group.

One of the first news articles printed was
on April 6, 1991. Back on page 7b a small

article stated "Little Rock citizens lend muscle to drug war; DIGNITY patrol high crime area."

The article reported about a group of black men (Muslims) who have begun patrolling a portion of central Little Rock to fight drug-related crime. It said they will continue to do so indefinitely.

Quoting Muslim and DIGNITY member J.B. Muhammad, "The community has been fearful of the drug dealers for too long because of strong-arm tactics. Area residents tired of the crime cheered the group's efforts and offered assistance."

"I can understand what the Muslims are doing and all that's good. Black men have a negative look and the Muslims are being good role models, trying to do something to help the community," said Jessie, a woman who requested her real name be withheld because of threats towards her. She said her home had been burglarized twice since November 1990 and her calls to police have resulted in threats against her."

Her family has lived in the house at Wright Avenue and Marshall Street a block from the Masjid since the 1920's. "My mother lived here as a child, my sister was born in this house and now I live here".

"What gets me is this was once a middle-class neighborhood where educators and businesspeople lived, and now it's

mixed with the negative element. The
drugs and crime have taken over the
neighborhood." The article continues
with Muhammad reporting the scary
threats made by drug dealers toward the
group that have many of them scared.

We're not vigilantes but the police can't
do it all. We're responsible community
members who've taken action.

Muhammad warns though if anyone comes at us the wrong way, we will defend ourselves.

The article correctly clarifies that the group includes members of other religions, and that our efforts are not religion-sponsored. Our purpose for the patrols in which DIGNITY members talk to those loitering is the first phase of behavior modification but quickly added the next would include surveillance and intelligence gathering and to expose drug terrorists with the information being passed on to the police.

The newspaper Arkansas Democrat even conducted an opinion poll asking the public if they backed the efforts of such civilian drug patrols such as a group known as DIGNITY?

These few articles did help us gain some immediate attention in Little Rock. The news papers quickly sought comments from the local police department spokesman about the patrols.

Little Rock Police Chief Louis Caudell and officers assigned to the area admitted that the area was in the middle of the city's highest crime zones. They welcomed the extra help as long as those in the group did not follow vigilante tactics. The article concluded by saying "DIGNITY appears to represent vigilance and concern; both in short supply of city leadership in attacking the gang and drug problems."

The following Monday we scheduled a meeting with Chief Caudell and Assistant Chief Randy Reed in which four members of the group discussed mutual concerns and sought ways to reach a better understanding of how to cooperate with the police.

Caudell welcomed the "citizen involvement" if members didn't become overzealous.

"They know the neighborhood, aren't easily intimated so we anticipate no problems so long as they notify us when they need to."

Associate Editor Deborah Mathis wrote in her column about black pride on the rebound with an idea that is not new. Reaching into the past to the battle cry "Black Power" when taken as a call to insurrection.

She wrote that we operated on the principal to instill the can-do spirit, to reclaim responsibility proving to the world that despite what it thinks, we have what it takes. Moreover, prove it to ourselves. No one gets hurt.

She ended her story stating that she hoped this time America is ready for it.

Now on alert of our purpose the police made themselves a very visible presence whenever we went on our night patrols never interfering always remaining close by. Somewhat bolstered by their presence and the public now aware of who we are the group increased significantly as more people who wanted to support us or just curious began showing up.

Some asked questions about the organization, others wanted to come out and just walk with us. By mid April as it got warmer, as many as seventy people especially on the weekends would show up and walk the patrol with us until around midnight.

We welcomed the support and the attention. It was a beautiful sight to see that many people both men and women joining to support this community effort.

On what is becoming but never a complacent typical patrol, on the parking lot of Braswell Barbecue at 1702 Wright Avenue. About a dozen men would loiter when the building closed at night.

They joked and laughed at us on this sticky spring evening. None of them paid much attention to the "No Loitering" sign the owner had put up. But when three men in black jump suits, web belts, ball caps and combat boots approached the loiterers would melt away grudgingly now displaced. They are men of DIGNITY and that was the effect we hope to have on those whose activities lead too often to fighting, drug dealing or sometimes worse.

Local resident Greg Warren welcomed patrol members as they entered his father's washateria at 1815 Wright Avenue. Warren said his father had asked him to discourage the drug dealers but they returned later to smash their windows in retaliation.

Greg stated that in ten years in business, that was the first real problem but it's cleaned up since the patrols started.

He also complimented the police for now being more noticeable too. We used to have a fight here almost every day. Our efforts quickly impress those in the community.

Established and more well-known leaders in the community started showing up to walk with us on the nightly patrols. Now bolstered by the spotlight on DIGNITY, people like Little Rock Municipal Judge Marion Humphrey actually joined the group. Little Rock City Director John Lewellen and civil rights attorney John Walker came out and walked on some of the Friday night patrols.

John Walker believes the citizens are the real victims. The majority of our people are law bidding citizens who wish to live in peace and harmony without being physically or mentally assaulted by those who engage in drug use and distribution.

He sees that DIGNITY is approaching the problem compassionately and sensitively. This is a community problem which extends racial, economical and geographical lines and must be attacked in that manner. Attorney Walker added DIGNITY sent the message that "we do care, more than we get credit for caring."

John Lewellen said he's lived in the neighborhood twenty-seven years and this is really the heart of the black community.

It's not the prosperous community it once was when people could walk the streets with their children or the elderly. Lewellen said that DIGNITY had made a significant difference. I've personally seen an increase level of safety the people feel.

Even Little Rock police officers D. Jackson and Mike Horton said "we like them". "Our call load is so heavy, we can't be here all the time", and "their presence out here just intimidates these people selling drugs.

New DIGNITY member Robert Jones who also lives close by recalled that a few nights earlier a prostitute told DIGNITY that they were messing up her game but a day later the same woman ran to us for help. She is not on the streets tonight.

He further added that before the patrols the police were rarely seen. They didn't see us caring for ourselves but since the police have been nearby the drug and violence activity has been curtailed significantly. Robert also stated "we are watching individuals go back to slavery and we are letting the drug addicts know that we love you but you are our enemy."

We can't stop people from smoking crack in their homes but our message is "get off the streets and not in front of our children".

It's now June and there is a major difference in the loitering, drug use activity, violence and crime in our six block patrol area. We began changing our schedule from patrolling every day and set up a schedule for those of us who work full time during the day.

Anywhere from 6 to 15 people would march up and down Wright Avenue on different nights six days a week but we did not march on Sundays. Even God rested after six days of work.

Sunday would be our day of restoration.

Then the incredible happened. On June 20, 1991 Arkansas Governor Bill Clinton and first lady, Hillary joined us on patrol which means we now have the attention of the entire state watching us. Made honorary member, the governor is now wearing our hat and he patrolled Wright Avenue with us. He publicly brought support to our cause on this night and it also meant even more police including the State Police. This action displaced significant criminal activity within a six-block radius for days.

Clinton told the press he and his wife read about us and were impressed with what we are doing.

"They are an unusual coalition of minority business, educators, Christians and black Muslims, all of whom believe that the community has a responsibility to solve some of its own problems". "In patrolling those streets and trying to find constructive things for those children to do and trying to run off people who are selling drugs or otherwise doing illegal things, I think they are serving a valuable purpose".

"I think it has the promise of really changing culture in Little Rock's inner city and elsewhere nationally".

So impressed with our purpose and seeing our commitment, that very Friday Governor Clinton released $15,000 from

his personal use emergency fund to
DIGNITY in its fight to hold down crime
and to expand our message into other
communities.

Now that Clinton has added his full
support each day we are getting more
and more publicity from the news paper
agencies around the country, local
television stations began assigning

crews to give reports daily on our activities and crime fighting adventures.

Clinton a consummate professional began making political statements about convening state and local leader's summits to address the problem.

Even national and state publications like Crime Beat and the Arkansas Times came out to do stories on the organization.

In July at the request of the Arkansas Democrat, the Little Rock police separated and compiled crime figures on an approximately five-square block radius surrounding the intersection of Wright Avenue and Wolfe Street, our patrol zone.

Statistics of police activity in that area between April 1 and June 30, 1991 were compared to figures for the same period in 1990. Statistics show that overall crime was down by twenty-two percent from 1990.

A detailed breakdown shows there were reductions in reports of drug activity, loitering, public intoxication, fights and disturbances – all offenses DIGNITY targeted!

Officers were called sixty-one fewer times in the area which translated to about sixty man hours saved. The biggest change noted was the number of disturbances which decreased to 16 from

82 reports and narcotics calls fell to four from eleven.

Lt. Stuart Thomas administrative officer that compiled the report stated the DIGNITY patrols are successful and doing the right thing which is stemming crime growth in central Little Rock.

"Either they are handling them or they're running them off". Sgt. Steve Archer who has patrolled Wright Avenue for five years commended the group and its efforts.

The difference is unbelievable. Archer who initially feared the group's motives said those concerns are now gone. "They serve as our eyes and ears; instead of acting on their own, they quickly contact us when they see potential crime situations."

Not everyone though is singing our praises.

One Friday night on patrol as we approached two men suspected of making a drug deal, they fled discarding behind bushes what was later determined to be crack cocaine. The guys got away but were no longer seen back in the neighborhood.

Someone not pleased ripped down some of our prevention flyers we put up declaring the neighborhood area a drug free zone.

DIGNITY founder Bernard Murray shared that even the Masjid members have noticed a considerable drop-off of people involved in criminal activity.

He attributed our success to God's Grace and our non-vigilante tactics in preventing crime in the area but added that we will still defend ourselves if needed, but we're not the aggressors.

Chapter Four
What is D.I.G.N.I.T.Y.?

If it bleeds, it leads. I don't know where that term originated from but from the daily violence it very well could have been in Little Rock.

The competing two newspapers and three television stations are making their fortunes selling newspapers and selling advertisements running lead stories depicting the violent mainly black-on-black crime that is occurring in Little Rock on an hourly basis.

Crime in Little Rock really was big business for some people. But here comes DIGNITY! A small group of concern black men of faith willing to put their lives on the line for a moral stand in a small but extremely important section in Little Rock. Actually patrolling, watching and encouraging better behavior among their own children and neighbors.

After reporting yet another grisly shooting or act of violence on the streets local news commentators on the TV began to make off-the cuff jokes and sarcastic remarks. Listing other locations around the city where we were needed that DIGNITY could patrol as they led into another story of what DIGNITY was doing.

The group was also now gaining popularity from our many requests to prevention assemblies in the local schools.

Within a mile of the intersection of Wright Avenue & High Street, a historically and predominantly black neighborhood is the Arkansas State Capitol. Nearby is Baptist Hospital, one of the largest medical hospitals in the city.

Barton Coliseum where the annual fair, shows and major concerts occurred is in walking distance. Plus there is the internationally famous Central High

School and historic Dunbar Junior High School which has its own dramatic history.

The Dunbar Community Center now sits at the former home site of J.E. Bush an associate of Booker T. Washington and his son John & Alice Bush III representing five generations of educators and prominence in the black community.

Nearby are two historical black colleges Arkansas Baptist College and Philander Smith College. The world-renowned Children's Hospital and the Governor's Mansion are also mere blocks away.

L.C. and Daisy Bates lived two blocks away. For me this was the neighborhood I grew up in, my neighborhood, period!

I personally knew many of these people as neighbors, friends, lovers, employers, disciplinarians, mentors, competitors and they were people respected, educated, resourceful and competent.

My mother Fannie Lou Butler was the Registrar at Arkansas Baptist College.

I was also an original member of the sixties radical group called the Black United Youth (BUY) lead by Bobby Brown and Robert Broadwater.

There were plenty of places to get great food to eat, nearby ball fields for football and baseball, basketball courts, the boys club, Carver YMCA; all of these things were within a short walking distance. My childhood was great growing up on these streets.

So I felt compelled to do whatever it took to reclaim my dignity in my neighborhood.

I would no longer just stand by watching these kids dying by the hundreds everyday on the same streets where I used to find comfort.

In the late sixties as a member of Black United Youth I stood on the picket lines in front of Kroger and Safeway grocery stores just blocks away facing the all-white establishment fighting for better jobs and equality for our people. How could I not take the same risk for these kids? We fought hard and risked our safety back then for jobs and equality on these streets.

Now on these same streets there were too many of our kids' fast becoming prey to the debilitating cheap crack cocaine now accessible. A source of unheard of volumes of quick money did not allow for the vision of hard work to develop ethics that we fought for without the action of those like the men of DIGNITY willing to stand firm.

Through DIGNITY I thought we could help provide a direction if we could only stay consistent and vigilant.

There is also something more personal for me and that is to provide some direction and responsibility to my own baby brother who too had fallen prey to crack cocaine and is dying, but that's another story for another time.

Yes, we are our brother's keeper.

My humble beginnings started in a place known as Dark Hollow across the Arkansas River in North Little Rock March 1954. My parents Lawrence Clayborn (LC) & Fannie Lou Butler were lifelong residents of the Little Rock area and some of my first memories are when we later moved and lived in a duplex at 1411 N. Ringo Street.

Ringo Street was one of most regularly traveled pedestrian streets because it was a straight walk or drive north and south for thirty-three straight blocks to the very southern end of town. A lot of Little Rock's influential blacks lived on or close to Ringo St.

Dunbar High School later Dunbar Junior High School is on 18th & Ringo St.

Dunbar Community Center and Gibbs the elementary school I attended is on 16th & Ringo.

Beginning at 14th Street was Mrs. Marshall's Confectionary Store where I started working at age seven bagging sandwiches and confectionary treats.

The confectionary was cookies, candies, chips, soda pop, pickles and ice cream. I made about seventy-five cents a shift and whatever sandwich and drink I wanted. Mrs. Marshall was a very nice lady with two older daughters who were away at college. Living two houses away made it easy for me to commute.

Just across the street was my church Mount Pleasant Missionary Baptist. One of the largest, oldest and influential black churches in Little Rock with Reverend Wesley E. Hayes as senior pastor.

Martin Luther King and many black national dignitaries visited our church.

At the other corner of the block on 15th St. was Taylor's Cleaners and behind it was Mr. Mansker's Barbershop.

From the time I was seven years old I lived right in the middle of daily opportunities to earn money doing various chores for my neighbors.

My grandmother Jerushia Trowser was the best seamstress and tailor in the area, making and altering dresses, coats and suits for many black and white people in Little Rock. She lived at 1413 Ringo St. just two houses from us.

My grandmother was a self-employed entrepreneur and she did specialty sewing for most of the local black and white cleaners and clothing stores. I spent many a day helping her in my youth, pinning, outlining and cutting fabric patterns, picking up the scrap cuttings, which would later be made into a patch quilt or something else usable.

My grandmother would make specially fitted dress suits for a lot of the harder to fit men in the city and for the women, dresses for special occasions. She also prepared hot lunches for the men and customers at the nearby barbershops, ACME Cleaners employees and Dunbar Community Center staff.

She earned a good living never asking anyone for help. But as I grew older I became too macho and masculine for sewing, "big boys don't sew."

If only I knew then what a good tailor or fashion designer makes today.

One of my best friends during the early and mid sixties was Michael Taylor who lived in the same duplex next door. Mike was about two years older than I am and his grandparents owned Taylor's Cleaners across the street, a long established family owned cleaners. His mother Ruth a divorcee, worked as a registered nurse at Baptist hospital.

As teens, Mike and I worked at the shine parlor that was in the cleaners which allowed us to make good and steady money.

We learned how to spit shine and polish the Highway State Troopers black boots and most of the other law enforcement guys were dropping their shoes off to be polished by us. We charged seven dollars a pair which was a lot of money even for us back in those days but the shine would last a week and scuffs easily buffed out with only a little water.

Ever the hustler I did not know the word entrepreneur back in those days.

When I was about ten or eleven years old I began cutting yards during the spring and summer months. My services were unique from the other kids who also cut grass because I also edged the sidewalks, swept the front and back porch and raked up my clippings for the same price. Sometimes my dad would help me the first time to make the yard look perfect. Afterwards I just basically kept them maintained which was a snap completing jobs timely. A lot of my extra money came from the tips for a well-done job. After a while I was cutting all the yards around my block and most in the neighborhood plus I provided another service a lot of people did not do.

I learned how to hand-wax hardwood floors.

A lot of the larger homes had hardwood floors. I painstakingly on my knees would hand apply the floor wax to the wood and with a buffer would bring a shine that lasted all year.

Another money making venture I started was selling JET magazines. During those days the JET magazine was a vital information link for national news in the local black communities. But for some reason only a few were sold and infrequently at the local barber and beauty shops.

My business was a door-to-door weekly service.

I brought your JET magazine to your house to read sometimes while I cut your grass.

It was a good business that I did until I was about fourteen. The Jet magazine cost me eighteen cents and I charged twenty-eight cents. A lot of times my customers would give me thirty cents or more and tell me to just keep the change.

This allowed me the opportunity growing up to pay for the majority of my clothes, the movies and other stuff I wanted without hassle from my parents.

But it was reading the magazine that awakened the writer in me. The first published article I ever wrote is in a Jet magazine. My grandmother taught me how to sew, so during the late sixties I made money selling African Dashikis for $15 each when we became Afro-Americans and started singing James Brown's "I'm Black and I'm Proud."

One of the first things that impressed me about this collection of black men was the complete lack of ego among us. All of us brought similar but different talents that meshed in spiritual harmony. For the first time in a long time I felt I was among men of purpose and determination. We meshed into a zone of comfort which allowed the flow for discussion of common goals, the reason we are here, what we want to accomplish and is it possible? Roles within the organization quickly established without rancor or dispute.

I guess we all were praying for the same thing.

We came together with common cause to face a danger without any personal knowledge of one another and quickly organized with the efficiency and purpose of a "trained military unit." It was that look that we went with.

DIGNITY though never would have made the immediate impact that it did if not for the participation and involvement of vice-president and co-founder Bill Walker Jr. For him to take on this type of initiative to combat drugs, gangs and violence in this fashion gained us the immediate attention of the press and government officials.

I greatly admired his courage to put at risk his own political career and personal safety on a daily basis to attempt to rescue a community where he too grew up. For such a young man he had an air of confidence about him that many people quickly mistook as arrogance, which is a behavior I too am sometimes accused of exhibiting. I've always felt confident in my abilities to adapt in most situations that sometimes people mistook as arrogance. I knew the good boys but I knew bad boys too. You tend to comingle with all types growing up. Acceptance by my peers was depending on who I was dealing with because sometimes I had good and bad tendencies too.

Bill had that same comfort zone with people. He was shrewd and successful but still had that street appeal. If he could successfully pull this off, it would cement his foundation in this community and his legacy in the city where he wanted to live. It was his DIGNITY that made the difference in how we were viewed in the community.

Our president and co-founder Jamal
Safee-Ullah, owner of Jamal's Import a
retail store at 1306 Wright Avenue. He
sold popular clothing that attracted
many of the young people with fancy
cars and big money they made from the
streets.

He wanted his business to be successful
but he also wanted pride and self-respect
in the community. He grew up in poverty
living in Blytheville, Arkansas with
eleven brothers and sisters. He'd joined
the Army as a cook seeking a better life.
Now at age 41 and a Muslim worshiper at
the nearby Masjid Ameen Zakariya,
Jamal thinks the core Muslim following is
the group's strength. Most of them have

experienced the drug culture in some form. They know how drugs break the family up and break down self-esteem because some of them are still trying to reclaim parts of their lives. Like most of us he too had brothers that had been users of crack cocaine.

Jamal's vision for DIGNITY was to expand its focus to eventually promote economic development in the downtrodden neighborhoods and find creative stimulating jobs providing alternatives to using and selling drugs.

Another co-founder and board member Bernard Murray, the originator of the term DIGNITY is a native of Baltimore who grew up in North Carolina. A

Muslim and recently married he purchased a house in the Quapaw Quarters an integrated neighborhood of expensive homes in the historic downtown residential portion of Little Rock. Lawyers, Doctors and professionals who worked downtown lived in these well maintained homes for convenience and realty investments. Studying engineering in college he also boxed professionally for a few years. When he moved to Little Rock he started his own construction business and worked part-time as a concert promoter. He is the father of two sons but they lived out of state. Bernard is a strong believer in Islam, a religion he sees where race is no concept. He sees the thieves and drug dealers as society dividers for selfishly working for their own destructive profit rather than for the good of everyone. He grew up in a stable home with both parents who were small business owners and he's never used drugs.

Bernard and I are the same age and we quickly bonded over the months and soon became good friends. We both played chess and he loved to debate different religious ideologies. He is reflective when he speaks as someone who reads a lot. His approach is direct and to the point. Another similarity I found appealing.

Original member Reverend Rickey Hicks
is the pastor of Connor Chapel African
Methodist Episcopal Church, a
personable man of deep faith and
wisdom in spite of his obvious youthful
appearance. Rickey is not a large man in
stature but appears to be a man that
stands his ground. A native of Strong,
Arkansas he launched a similar
grassroots campaign there. Now a
successful lawyer and small
businessman he was financially secure
and far removed from the scenes of
everyday street life happening on Wright
Avenue. I assumed that maybe he was
influenced by the many funerals the
churches were holding daily for our dead
children, or maybe it was the many

clients coming into his law office affected by crime that motivated him. Whatever his reasons were, Rickey stood side-by-side with this unique collection of religious men to embark upon something that would be special not only for this neighborhood but for the entire city of Little Rock.

Another founding member is Johnny Hasan. Johnny, the Imam of Masjid Ameen Zakariya a spiritual leader, is someone I did not know as being from Little Rock. Though born in Little Rock, Johnny grew up in Detroit graduating from Southeastern High School. Growing up in Detroit his drug experience was with heroin and marijuana. He returned to live in Little Rock in 1973 where he accepted Al-Islam. He now lives in a house nearby off of 18th & High Street and "he gives back" working as a drug counselor and health education director for community based agencies.

He is involved in correctional ministry for state and federal prisons contracted as a chaplain and certified religious assistant. He and I have similar employment backgrounds working in social services helping and counseling others. Johnny and I spent many nights and some days patrolling the neighborhoods and we attended many other events together on behalf of the organization. He usually spoke last after hearing what had been said by others either to offer his opinion in agreement or disagreement. A quiet man respected by all of the Muslims with which he spoke.

I too learn to trust him completely and we patrolled together sometimes when we worked in the smaller groups.

Muhammad Rasheed grew up in North Little Rock at Eastgate Terrace, a housing project with a reputation for many violent deaths of young males and intense gang activity. Muhammad spent four years in the United States Air Force as a fuel specialist. He says the military provided him an escape and saved him

from the streets of Dark Hollow an area
well known for the very poor blacks who
lived there. After military, Muhammad
earned a degree in Louisiana in
adolescent behavior working in youth
homes and briefly for the Job Corps.
Now at age 36 Muhammad says people
around him corrupted by cocaine
motivates him to come out. A Muslim
who has been in many organizations
found DIGNITY hits home for him. He is
employed at a printing company during
the day and now spends his nights on
patrol. He believes the fact that several
of us have military backgrounds
provides the discipline for the
organization's success.

Besides our connection to Dark Hollow, I too served in the US Air Force ironically also an administrative specialist in Fuels and Munitions for the 366th F-14 fighter jet squadron at Mountain Home, Idaho. Muhammad also noted the time, energy and sacrifice that affects his job and family when he makes the daily patrols. But for him the effort is worth the risk; it's more than stomping out drugs, it's about jobs for kids and putting DIGNITY back in the neighborhoods.

Yusuf Ali, perhaps the eldest of this group, is in his mid-fifties. Originally from Hope, Arkansas, incidentally the same hometown as our governor, Bill Clinton. He moved to Los Angeles,

California as a child. He became a Muslim while in prison after a long life of crime. He became addicted to both heroin and cocaine. He was also doing other things that were not becoming of a Muslim. He is divorced with three children whose ages range from 34, 18 and 5 who are in California. Yusuf came to Little Rock less than a month ago to, in his words, "get away and start anew" to fight against the very things he used to do. He recently participated in a month-long fast with members at the Masjid. He earns an honest living wherever he can sometimes with Bernard in his construction business or other members of the mosque. With the patrols now going into the schools to talk to the children he finds it is satisfying for him and allows him to make amends for an amoral lifestyle.

He compared his participation to being a "leaf on the tree".

Yusuf an original board member is quickly dubbed the "philosopher" of the group because of the wisdom he displayed to those on the streets he encountered while on patrol.

I appreciated his calm gentle demeanor and the way he interacted with people. He was a natural who wasted that valuable talent in his youth to get over on people to live a criminal lifestyle. I could sense his repentance and effort to make amends.

Prayer, fasting and supplication will do that for you.

Then there is Robert Jones who joined the organization maybe a few days after we started the patrols. A tax enforcement officer for the State Department of Labor, Robert owns a home near Wright Avenue, married, the father of a son and daughter both approaching adulthood. A Baptist from New Orleans he was stationed at Little Rock Air Force Base in 1963 where he met his wife and decided to stay and raise his family in Little Rock. After being discharged from the military, working as a janitor and bricklayer he earned his college degree at Philander Smith College studying business administration. He's never used cigarettes, drugs or alcohol and he tries never to use profanity. He watched as the neighborhood steadily declined over the years. Beginning with the influx of youth being bused out and dropped off from places like California and Chicago for the sole purpose of setting up gangs to sell drugs. "When I looked out of my window I saw carloads of kids on the street selling drugs, prostituting and shooting all night long. I felt, "Whose fault will it be if something isn't done?" "It will be mine if I don't take an active part".

He too prayed as we all did for an answer.

Then he spotted DIGNITY one night on patrol and knew immediately he had to join up. Robert is perhaps the most animated member of all when speaking his messages of concern and giving inspiration. To me he was that Pentecostal deacon that is always part of the praise ministry that gets everybody on their feet and into the spirit.

He and I shared how our wives were worried about our safety while on patrol. He too instinctively felt as if God drew him there as a voice to speak to all concerned and to reach into their mental consciousness to help them see the negativity of what is happening to them. Robert was welcomed as a member of DIGNITY and as a board member.

Emanuel Muhammad is someone I knew most of my life growing up but he was older. He is closer in age to my half-sister Barbara but I saw him many times in the neighborhood with people we both knew over the years. Emanuel on Saturdays would set up his smoker and sold food in front of the Masjid which drew a lot of business for him from friends. He had a smoke-link sandwich which seemed to draw me there regularly at least a couple times a month. Married with a family he lived nearby.

There of course would be others who would join at different intervals that made significant and critical contributions to DIGNITY.

They will be noted when due but this basically was the core group that started the DIGNITY organization.

Prayer, faith in God plus collective action equals difference.

We had the spiritual balance we needed.

It is now mid July and its hot and sticky but so far, so good. Not one person has been threatened, shot at, injured or taken to jail from any action occurring while DIGNITY is on patrol. However there is now a very noticeable change, a very pleasant change in the environment in how people now feel.

There is some comfort to come out into their yards or take a walk around the block, especially at night along Wright Avenue.

I believe starting our patrols during early spring months before it got hot actually helped us get prepared for the summer. By now we have patrolled the area almost every day for eight weeks, the people are now fully aware of who we are and what our purpose is. Local dignitaries aware of our actions from the press now come out for nightly walks with us.

Many including our governor had come out in support of our mission and the local press is now doing more individual reports on some of our members introducing them to the community.

But most importantly crime is down and no one has been shot or killed under our watch.

In fact the change was so substantial that the patrols became more staggered, we worked in smaller groups, the use of video cameras and flash lights were less obvious as we established positive relationships with the business owners. We adapted and became less obtrusive but still visible.

While we knew what we were doing was not unique because of well known groups all over the country like the Guardian Angels and others in larger cities waging similar battles in their neighborhoods. As positive thinking men we knew we had to continue to bring proactive ideas and show creative leadership to the city as a whole. We also knew to be able to accomplish the things important to us, we needed to access every public medium out there to gain the ultimate attention necessary to further instill our point of view upon the consciousness of the people. We began looking at and identifying other hot spots closer to where we lived in Little Rock to expand and begin new patrols.

Our relationship with local law enforcement and its leadership has improved to a friendly status and before school ended for summer we went into several other neighborhood schools with our anti-gang anti-drug prevention messages. More people were requesting our caps and t-shirts to wear in support.

If we can claim six blocks why not claim our whole city?

DIGNITY would then have established its own special history in Little Rock folklore.

Chapter Five
Dick Gregory Finds
DIGNITY in Little Rock

Today is Monday July 22ⁿᵈ and God makes the impossible possible.

Civil rights activist and comedian Dick Gregory is in Little Rock as the guest of Deborah Robinson director of Storer Cable's Black Access channel 14 talk show to speak on race relations. It is her show's 10th anniversary and taping that same day.

Dick was not there for DIGNITY nor was he even aware of our group. However he did know Bill Walker Jr. from his frequent travels as a teenager with Bill's father William L. "Sonny" Walker Sr. a noted Arkansas civil rights leader in the sixties. He later became the first black man to hold an important state office under then Gov. Winthrop Rockefeller as director of the state Office of Economic Development.

The senior Walker then became one of the highest-ranking blacks when he was named regional director of the federal Community Services Administration during President Richard Nixon's era.

Dick had not come to Little Rock to make it his next stage in his own well-known drug battle crusade and when Bill approached him he was reluctant because of the many other similar crusades he'd led in various communities around the country. The most recent being a 1989 seven-month anti-drug campaign in Shreveport, Louisiana spending hundreds of thousands of his own money.

He did not want our DIGNITY patrols to be trivialized by his celebrity presence. But Bill was able to convince him to come to the DIGNITY office, meet the marchers and then make a decision.

I believe he respected the fact that here is this young black state legislator out there putting everything he had on the line to save lives in his community.

Dick too was looking for something and God would reveal it to him.

As we gathered together for that evening's patrol Jamal told us not to go out until Bill arrived. No one knew actually what was going on since no one had seen nor talked to Bill or Rickey that day but Jamal would only say that Bill wanted us all there that night.

Then about 8:30 Bill drove up in his new blue Jaguar, Rickey trailing in his blazer. As they walked in I immediately noticed the other man with them as a familiar man, and famous face.

It is Dick Gregory.

As he, Rickey and Bill entered the small room the men quickly stood up, and greeted him. Each of us stood to shake his hand while briefly introducing ourselves.

Bill and Rickey both are giving us that look of mission accomplished.

The headquarters is nothing extravagant or even set up like an office. It is just a few tables and chairs, no air conditioning with only a ceiling fan moving hot air around and a small toilet. But for now it is our place to meet up, organize and go.

But somehow that night the room transformed into something spiritual because here is a great man of knowledge bringing to a group of men very receptive to that knowledge.

It was almost as if we were now being anointed and he is this guru coming amongst us to give the necessary inspirational go-get-em.

He sat in a chair but he never stayed seated for long. Here standing before us was an American icon. Someone we watched all of our lives from afar and respected from the civil rights movement, an originator of personal dignity and someone who knew and marched with the late Dr. Martin Luther King himself. I was in awe just to be in his presence, but he quickly put us at ease with his demeanor and the way he spoke to us. He quickly became one of us, I think he felt it too especially when he was presented a DIGNITY cap that he immediately placed on his head.

That night Dick went out on patrol with us with about a dozen men, regulars who are now the main core of DIGNITY. Gregory 58, in slacks, patent leather shoes, African style pullover and now proudly displaying his new DIGNITY cap.

With his whitish beard, slender ascetic build, plus the obvious deference shown to him, he had the air of a prophet.

We then prepared for the nights patrol. Displaying a new sign that stated **"DIGNITY means no *Rocks* in Little Rock"** with word rocks in large red letters, a ragged line formed in the parking lot between Jamal's and the DIGNITY office.

In our full black regalia, flashlights and walkie-talkies and video rolling we began this patrol with a new purpose. With Bill and Dick up front leading we began our customary walk up Wright Avenue. Purposefully chanting "Down with Dope, Up with Hope" we strutted proudly.

An added new face in the group, Dick Gregory generated more than the usual attention to the patrol this night. People who normally just blow their horns or wave support quickly recognized we had someone special with us. They quickly found places to park along the route some even wanted to join the patrol. Other than the immediate attention in the neighborhood his presence drew there is little criminal activity to report this evening. The Ebony Club had even closed down early and apart from a few stragglers outside of Braswell Barbecue there were very few loiters. After patrolling for almost five months the drug dealing and gang activity had relocated into other neighborhoods.

The patrol is now almost a victory walk. W.E. B. Dubois talked about the talented tenth' who had returned back to the community and brought along the rest. It was important for those of us who had "gone off and got educated" to become professionals to return to these neighborhoods and give something back.

The problem of education then among blacks must first of all deal with the Talented Tenth; it is the problem of developing the best of this race that they may guide the mass away from the contamination and death of the worst in their own and other races.

The patrol concluded about midnight but our work is just beginning.

We returned back to the office after about three hours of patrolling. Dick gave his assessment of what he saw and felt about the patrol. After sitting around talking until 3 A M Dick found out that he was with guys who were witty, clever and committed.

He thought maybe he found what he was looking for right here with us, a family.

Many would question his alliance with DIGNITY because of larger cities with similar problems but what he found here with DIGNITY was a model for other bleeding cities to heal themselves. He would utilize many of the same tactics he used in Shreveport but this time he had DIGNITY's religious non-violent approach plus our positive community appeal aiding him. For us that three or four hours transfixed all of us in a way none of us could immediately comprehend but with the knowledge and directions he shared with us, our focus on our mission can be even more effective to combat drugs, gangs and the violence in Little Rock. His words flowed with the majesty and purpose of a shaman. As the meeting winded down Reverend Rickey Hicks gave a fervent prayer of consecration towards our future journey in this struggle.

DIGNITY will now immediately begin a series of high profile initiatives that will affect not only Little Rock but the entire state. Dick stated he was also there to patrol with us for as long as it took. We now had a new center of focus, some creative bold new ideas to promote our message and a nationally known celebrity; a civil rights activist now involved to help us. His personal assistant Reginald "Reggie" Toran arrived in town and is now also present.

Our first attack would be against the businesses that profit legitimately selling drug paraphernalia and rolling papers, items that promote and glamorize the use of drugs. I suggested that we target Armadillo's Hands, a well known head shop in Little Rock. Armadillo's Hands owner Joe Frawley is someone I knew from high school. His parents apparently had money and helped him set up his business. Joe also made a lot of money selling mainly high quality pot while we were in high school and shortly after graduating he opened a small head shop selling all of the things that young people buy like black lights, strobe lights, posters, ceiling nets, incense and of course all kinds of exotic drug paraphernalia. He later added expensive leather biker clothing such as jackets and pants, sexy women's leather clothing, bikinis, tie-dyed t-shirts, jeans, sunglasses and jewelry. Joe is a diligent business man and made millions selling his non-conventional but popular products to teenagers, drug users, women, bikers and leather freaks. He later expanded to another store on 6318

Asher Avenue one of the busiest traveled streets in Little Rock.

The main reason I felt we needed to target Joe was the fact that everybody in Little Rock including law enforcement knew Joe unabashedly and openly without any scruples sold drug paraphernalia in his stores for almost twenty years. But when law enforcement make drug arrests on drug raids they always add the paraphernalia possession charge to pad the case, saying items sold legally are now illegal. I personally felt this was unfair enforcement of that particular law because the charge usually added more jail time for the minor offender.

I went to Armadillo's Hands shortly after it opened the next morning.

I wanted to purchase the drug paraphernalia from Joe himself. Sure enough there stood Joe behind the counter now much older but still wearing the same big red afro hairstyle that he had since we were teenagers. Over the years I admit I spent a lot of money buying popular items with Joe growing up in Little Rock but had not been in any of his stores in years since he moved to the main Asher Avenue store. After entering he greeted me with some odd familiarity but we did not renew old acquaintances.

I told him I was just looking around but was interested in a pair of sun shades. After browsing for several minutes I gradually made it back to an area in the rear of the store where he sold the drug items. He sold a variety and wide selection of pipes, hookahs, necklaces, clips and rolling papers. There is jewelry, key rings, medallions showing the marijuana leaf plus other accessories to enhance the drug experience. I purchased a small crack pipe, some screens, rolling papers and sunglasses.

I brought the items I bought back to the office. There, after a brief meeting, the decision was made to go back and confront Joe immediately asking him to stop selling drug paraphernalia out of his stores.

After hastily contacting a few reporters, Bill and Dick at a 1:30 PM press conference announced while displaying the items I purchased, that DIGNITY was going to Armadillo's Hands to ask for the immediate removal of those items we identified as being sold for drug use.

Dick holding up the glass pipe said the number one problem is not drugs but the fear of drugs and that drug paraphernalia should not be sold in this town. With reporters and photographers from all three Little Rock network television, both statewide newspapers and the State Press, the black newspaper in tow, DIGNITY and its newest member Dick Gregory made a sudden visit to Armadillo's Hands. We asked the owner who sold drug paraphernalia to remove the merchandise immediately and to place a sign we brought with us in his window apologizing to his customers for contributing to the drug problem in our city.

The sign also announced there will be no more drug paraphernalia sold here.

Joe was not there when we first entered the store. With Bill, Rickey and Dick leading the way followed by five other DIGNITY members along with the reporters and news cameras we entered the store. Several DIGNITY members remained outside. Bill and Dick approached the salesperson at the front counter introducing himself as state representative Bill Walker Jr. and a member of the organization DIGNITY.

He then stated the reason for our visit.

Startled by what was happening, the sales person was confused about what to do next, because now Dick Gregory was also introducing himself with the news cameras really bearing down to catch his every word.

The salesperson said that he was only an employee and would have to contact the owner. A phone call was made to Joe telling him what was happening. While

waiting for Joe to arrive there were
several customers inside. Being familiar
with the layout of the store I began
moving towards the back where Joe kept
the pipes and other smoking materials.
Getting Bill's attention I motioned to Bill,
Dick and the others directing them
towards me in the back of the store where
the glass cases containing the majority
of the paraphernalia was being openly
displayed.

Within five minutes Joe entered the store
refusing to give his name to reporters as
he stormed in angrily asking, "What is
the problem?"   Bill introduced himself
and Dick Gregory and explained the
reason for our visit. Bill then informed

Joe that we were here to ask him to remove the drug related items from his shelves. Joe asked the press to please stop filming and asked us all leave his store.

With the crowd of news media in his store Frawley said he sold the pipes only for tobacco use. Bill retorted "A lot of people sell this stuff and say it's for tobacco products. It's immoral" and again asked him to remove the pipes. Joe refused again asking everyone to leave his store.

Dick then said, "We'll leave when the pipes leave. That means today, tomorrow, next week or next year."

Joe then decided to close his store, we refused to leave. The stand-off would end when Joe became frustrated when no one would leave. He then pulled a shotgun from under the counter to intimidate us.

A DIGNITY member immediately left out of the store to a nearby pay phone and called the police. About 3:15 PM the first of five police cars arrived. Frawley was no longer displaying the shotgun when the officers entered the store and not realizing what was occurring talked to him first. Frawley told the officers that he did not want the protesters or media in his store.

The officers then talked with Bill who explained the reason why we were there.

The officers informed Bill and Dick that since the owner requested they leave the premises we would have to leave because a trespass complaint was now being reported by the property owner.

Refusing to comply with the police and with television cameras brightly glaring the officers contacted their supervisor attracting an additional police presence to the scene.

Given again the opportunity to leave and still refusing after almost half an hour the officers arrested Bill Walker Jr., Dick Gregory, Rickey Hicks, Kenneth Murray and David Dotson for criminal trespassing, a misdemeanor. Offering to give them citations with a court date, the men refused. Captain Sam Williams then led Bill, Dick and the others out the store walking in a single file holding their wrists crossed as if they were handcuffed. Bill following Dick's lead was escorted to the squad car. He bent over the hood of the car voluntarily offering to be frisked for weapons.

The entire event was videotaped by the three networks news stations for full dramatic affect for the evening news. They they were then transported to the police station. Police stated it wasn't illegal for Frawley as a business owner to have the shotgun in his store.

Upon arrival at the police department booking station Bill and Dick decided to remain in jail overnight until court the next morning while the others were issued citations and released.

Bill and Dick remained in jail overnight to make a symbolic statement about what DIGNITY represented, to increase the attention on the legal sales of drug paraphernalia and to appear in court personally on the trespass charge. At their arraignment escorted from the Little Rock city jail which again would have the press staked out watching their every move. They would leave the jail however about four hours later. Gregory, who was also already on a three-week hunger strike to protest the drug crisis was taken to St. Vincent Medical Infirmary Center after becoming dehydrated and fainted several times in his jail cell that night.

It was during this time my role in the group began to be more defined as the facilitator. I'm that foot soldier who worked behind the scenes out of the limelight to help our purpose and mission maintain its administrative continuity. I'm the one who identified Armadillo's Hands that sold the drug paraphernalia. I purchased the items shown to the press by Dick during the news conference. When we entered the store I directed them to the back of the store where the crack pipes were being sold. That day Dick Gregory's personal assistant Reggie Toran rode along with me to Armadillo's Hands and though we both were in the store that day, neither one of us was part of the group that would be arrested for trespassing. Reggie and I traveled in my car to the police department, back to the office, and to St. Vincent's Hospital when Dick took ill. I took him back to his hotel and picked him up for court that morning. DIGNITY members gathered at the hospital and remained together until ten-thirty that evening when it was reported that he was in stable condition. We held a brief prayer vigil and discussed strategy for the morning outside the hospital.

Early that Wednesday morning always one to capitalize on an opportunity at about seven-thirty the next morning Arkansas' Governor Bill Clinton paid a visit to St. Vincent's Hospital to see Dick Gregory. He quickly issued a press statement defending DIGNITY and their arrest for trespassing. The governor said DIGNITY members are basically law-abiding people. "What they're trying to do is highlight the role of people who are running apparently legitimate businesses who are providing and selling drug paraphernalia. I think it's part of an overall statement that it's the people in the community who are going to have to take responsibility for ridding the community of drugs. I'm very sympathetic with what they're trying to do." "I'm not going to work with them on breaking the law but I am going to work with them in trying to do whatever I can to help them eradicate drugs in the neighborhoods." "You have to look at it from their point of view, they're really afraid they're losing all their children and they're trying to do some things dramatically to highlight drug eradication." Clinton, issuing public comments prior to the court proceedings that would run on the early morning news shows, gave our pleas even more strength.

The governor also stated he visited Gregory to get some ideas for a meeting he convened with Little Rock, North Little Rock and Pulaski County government and school officials to address community violence that very morning.

The previous week Clinton met with city and county representatives to start studying the youth violence issue. Little Rock Mayor Sharon Priest called our actions as merely a form of protest and that she did not see our actions as a start of any great civil disobedience. There was only one complaint which came from a police department spokesman who stated that DIGNITY tied up a half-dozen police officers and valuable jail space in their grandstanding attempt to draw attention to the sale of purported drug paraphernalia and that the police department should not be used as a pawn for seeking publicity for individuals. Dick responded by saying that he is not trying to win a popularity contest with the police.

On July 24th the front page of the Arkansas Gazette splashed a huge picture that was captioned "Gregory goes to jail for DIGNITY" with a subtitle "Confrontation at Armadillo's Hands", the Arkansas Democrat's front page stated, "Lawmaker, Activist Arrested at LR Store" with a photo of Dick and Bill being led by police exiting the store appearing to be handcuffed.

All three television stations lead stories that morning began with video showing DIGNITY's leaders confrontation with Joe Frawley and then being arrested. The Little Rock community as a whole is now ripe for this type of positive energy, seeing black men standing strong seeking remedies to the violence, gangs and drugs.

The court appearance that morning would continue to have the same dramatic effect.

We gathered prior as a group at a designated location close by city hall, had prayer and then walked together the short distance to the courthouse.

Our numbers, our clothing and our now familiar profile is quickly spotted by the news media as we entered the building. It drew the attention of the many people driving to work or going to court on busy Markham Avenue. As we entered the court room people who are there for court, curiosity seekers, media and law enforcement now have the small court room filled to capacity. At nine that morning the five members of DIGNITY who were arrested, appeared in Little

Rock Municipal court for arraignment on the charge of criminal trespassing.

Municipal Judge Marion Humphrey now a member of DIGNITY and who walked the patrols with us recused himself and appointed local lawyer Jack Lassiter as a special judge to hear this case.

Attorneys John Walker and Rickey Hicks entered an innocent plea for the accused after Lassiter declined defense request to dismiss the charges. Dick Gregory insisted to be returned to jail until his trial to protest the open sale of drug paraphernalia but Lassiter declined to send Gregory to jail even after he refused to sign a form allowing his release on his own recognizance.

Gregory told Lassiter he wasn't trying to play games with the justice system but wanted to make a point and will continue to seek arrest until the city's drug problems are curbed. Lassiter order Bill, Dick and the others to return for trial Friday.

In the meantime on Wednesday instead of just complaining Little Rock narcotics officers served a search warrant at Armadillo's Hands and Ugly Mike's Records at 4708 W. 12th. Street another location given to police by DIGNITY. Officers seized items that police believe meet the definition for drug paraphernalia.

Mark Stodola, Pulaski County prosecuting attorney said the items taken from the stores are likely to bring drug paraphernalia charges against the owners. Stodola also mentioned that the pipes, vials, hand-held scales and others items seized at both stores are commonly used for marijuana, powder and crack cocaine. Later that day we held a 1:30 PM news conference at the headquarters of DIGNITY.

There Bill and Dick praised Arkansas lawmakers for the state law already in force prohibiting sale of specified drug paraphernalia and to urge other states to adopt a similar law.

Dick praising Bill also said that there was not another movement in the country where there is a politician involved that's out there every day doing what Bill is doing. Stating politicians and celebrities often patrol on a one-time basis and they definitely won't put their career and their body on the line every day like that. That's what makes this fight different. Dick realized quickly Little Rock really is different.

Meaning the difference is the commitment and the men he is working with. He said "The world will sit and look and say 'How did y'all do it?"

We then announced that we would indeed force another confrontation and return back to Armadillo's Hands to present Frawley with a copy of the anti-drug paraphernalia law. We also announced that we were expanding our direction into the corporate world that promotes the sale of paraphernalia and would present a letter to Kroger Foods threatening that if cigarette papers aren't taken off Little Rock shelves as activists we would publicly call for sit-down strikes at their stores nationwide.

Citing cigarette rolling papers sold by those stores are used to smoke illegal drugs.

Frawley on the other hand is no stranger of the 1981 Statute. Ten years prior he and nine other retailers filed a lawsuit challenging its constitutionality by contending the statute language was too vague but the 8th U.S. Circuit Court of Appeals upheld the law.

We arrived at his store a little after two with media in tow. Frawley politely accepted a copy of the law from Gregory but had harsh words for him when he refused the request to display a poster apologizing for selling drug paraphernalia.

"I don't want it. I'll put it in the garbage," Frawley said raising his voice. "I'm not going to put this in my store. Now do you want me to tear it up in front of your face?"

Having made our point we left the store before police, who Frawley this time called, arrived. Frawley then came outside and read a prepared statement as the media and DIGNITY stood by. "I believe in your cause and I know the community agrees. Our business has been in turmoil and I would appreciate it very much if you would leave so we can continue our business."

I sincerely support your efforts to get rock out of Little Rock.

If Joe Frawley and Armadillo's Hands can help DIGNITY stop the rock in Little Rock, we will walk with you." Frawley's offer to join DIGNITY in its effort to clear drug pushers off the streets led Gregory to ask if he was serious. Frawley assured him that he was but Dick took offense at Frawley's insistence that the pipes he was selling were legal products intended solely for tobacco use.

At least eighteen members of DIGNITY came out for patrol that Wednesday night.

The press now aware of Dick's first day of activities were chomping at the bit, following him all over town in their trucks, vans and cars to be on hand to witness DIGNITY's next move. His celebrity status of course now brought more scrutiny and criticism, but it also aroused curiosity. The stage was now set.

Tonight Dick led us in prayer reminding us of the parking lot fight that happened on Wright Avenue & High Street between rival gangs early Monday morning that led to the shooting of three youth.

The pace accelerated in such a way that we found ourselves busy trying to keep up with what was going on in this section of town. But the city was still reeling because of the recent highly publicized gang related killings of Jessie Faulkner on June 6th and when another community patroller Richard Campbell was shot from behind on July 10th in a section of downtown North Little Rock. It finally signified to government officials that the results of years ignoring the seriousness of gangs and violence associated with it.

More emphasis and effort was now being made by others, but here and now in our small office a group of concerned fed-up black men is making it known to the world that the fight to reclaim our neighborhoods is now being waged block-to-block if needed. Dick said it best, "When you take these turfs it's like a football game. It's not just about selling dope, it's like 'this is my turf' nobody is going to run us off these corners unless we are dead." "We're going to draw the line today with that brother, Jessie Faulkner who was killed". That night we were back patrolling Wright Avenue.

Restaurateur and local activist Robert 'Say' MacIntosh walked up, approached Dick and attempted to hand him a letter stating "Dick had until next Friday a week to get out of Little Rock with your political show." We ignored him and the patrol continued. Who Robert McIntosh is depends on who you ask about him. To some he is a civil rights leader. For others a hero, a blowhard, a lunatic, a character, a villain, a violent man, a philanthropist, an opportunist, a shill, a pioneer and an attention junkie drawn to the TV cameras as a moth is to a flame. The Say MacIntosh I knew was probably all of the above. He was a character who was always seeking attention so it was apropos that he would involve himself in some way even though he never came out one night to patrol with DIGNITY. Say did some nice things sometimes by handing out to poor children yearly at Christmastime dozens of bikes, dolls and other toys earning him the name as Little Rock's black Santa Claus. At the corner lot of 14th and High Street Say created a virtual cemetery, a very potent visual campaign to show the effects of gang violence. He placed small white crosses in the cemetery each one representing a young person killed in Little Rock that year. Sadly, that lot filled up fast.

Friday DIGNITY was again the lead story on all of the news networks and newspapers. It was also the day DIGNITY members returned to court for trial. We now had the attention of everyone statewide and gained national press attention.

Curiosity about the trial, intrigue about the organization and now some celebrity status with the populace, our influence in the community of showing ways to attack the violence was now taking on a life of its own with our local government leaders. Politicians looking to find something they could latch on are now showing interest in developing solutions to the problems. Many of them were watching to see if this independent group of men had solutions. For the trial to accommodate an unusually large crowd of curious spectators and media, defendants in other court matters were moved to the adjacent courtroom normally reserved for traffic court.

The large court room which could hold about 300 people was used. With the now ever present news media, faces of dozens of local dignitaries and community leaders such as Pulaski County Sheriff Carroll Gravett, his Chief Deputy Roy Hinson, and Reverend

Daniel Bowman were in attendance to witness the outcome.

The defendants, State Representative Bill Walker Jr., Civil Rights icon Dick Gregory, Reverend Rickey Hicks, Ken Murray and David Dotson were present for trial. Captain Sam Williams of the Little Rock Police testified that police responded to a trouble call Tuesday at Frawley's store.

He said Frawley asked them to evict the DIGNITY members.

The five were arrested after refusing to leave.

Frawley testified briefly. But on advice from his attorney, David Lewis, Frawley refused to answer any of attorney John Walker's questions except to say he owned the store and had asked the DIGNITY members to leave. Joe then invoked his Fifth Amendment right to freedom from self incrimination. After all testimony was given and members of DIGNITY did not refute the charges, Lassiter found the evidence against the members presented by Assistant Prosecuting Attorney Melody Noble sufficient to convict. The question was whether the state had proven criminal trespass. The state had met the burden of proof, but the judge found there were mitigating circumstances. The maximum punishment for the Class B misdemeanor was a $1,000 fine and a year in jail.

Lassiter fined each man $50 plus $78.25 in court costs, then suspended the fines on condition the men perform eight hours of community service "in some drug-related task." Immediately after the sentences were handed down John Walker told Lassiter "We'd like to have an order allowing them to be placed in jail rather than pay the fine."

Lassiter refused saying incarceration was not appropriate. Walker responded by saying he was notifying the court his clients may refuse to pay the fine. Not wanting to become further encumbered in this case the judge gave them 30 days to pay the fine, stating he was not going to put them in jail today. Outside the court room it was asked what DIGNITY achieved. Dick responded by saying, "The judge has his job to do and we have our job to do. If we're in the streets saying a drug free community is worth dying for, what was done today is to say it's also worth going to jail for."

Bill was asked if he feared the conviction would taint his legislative image, he replied "I am proud to be a part of the drug eradication movement" likening himself to Martin Luther King and Gandhi, men who promoted non-violent disobedience.

DIGNITY's next court stop that same morning was the Quorum Court room of the Pulaski County Courthouse just blocks away. There Governor Clinton had convened and was chairing his special called meeting with sixty government, church and community leaders to find ways to eradicate the causes of youth violence in central Arkansas.

Clinton cited a recent string of violent crime. The death of Richard Campbell and in the DIGNITY patrolled area on Wright Avenue where three youth were shot in a crowd of five hundred after midnight this past Monday. Coincidentally, the first night Dick patrolled with DIGNITY but after we left the area, led the governor to call the meeting.

Representatives of the law enforcement community stressed the need for more jail space for juveniles. Pulaski County Judge Floyd G. "Buddy" Villines said that the county could only house a maximum of twenty offenders and that they know the city does not have a place to put them.

Chief William P. Nolan of North Little Rock Police Department spoke of recently rearranging inmates to open a jail pod reserved for adults, to house three juveniles charged with felonies, including rape and multiple burglaries. Mark Stodola, Pulaski County prosecuting attorney said increasing jail space was only a "Band-Aid" solution and that the state needed to get serious about intervention measures. Rep. Bill Walker agreed that building jails was only a small part of the solution. Citing the need for community involvement, he used DIGNITY recent work as an example of prevention and educating people.

Ideas included regional boot camps for juveniles, increased jail space for juveniles, increased city-sponsored recreational activities and better code enforcement of substandard dwellings. Also to strengthen laws against selling alcohol to minors or buying it for them and to step up enforcement of laws that hold parents or guardians more accountable for their children's actions.

The governor urged the leaders to take the ideas into the community for feedback calling for another meeting in two weeks to refine the list. He also wanted to hear from youth who have been through the criminal justice system, was a key point that would motivate DIGNITY into action and brought up by City Director Lottie Shackleford. "Like everything else, you've got to get the people involved with the problem at the table and in the discussion. Dick warned not to concentrate solely on youth alone. "These young people are a reflection of us. Don't be so busy worrying about your young folks that you forget about the old folks." Clinton welcomed comments from anyone present and a wide variety of topics were discussed. Stronger penalties for youth arrested for carrying firearms is what the prosecuting attorney wanted.

He believed the laws left too much discretion in the hands of juvenile judges seeing young people only being shuffled through the system. "The next time I see them is when they commit a murder. Little Rock had seventy homicides in 1990 committed by youth between ages thirteen to seventeen. The governor asked him to meet with the two juvenile court judges and come up with a list of proposed law changes to be considered during legislative sessions. Mayor Priest and city manager Tom Dalton spoke in favor of placing non-uniformed resource officers in the junior and senior high schools but Municipal Judge Marion Humphrey opposed having police officers in the schools. He feared black youth would be treated more harshly than whites, especially if a confrontation involved black and white students.

Humphrey said there was a built-in friction between black males and the police. Again welcoming the judge's candor Governor Clinton said more blacks need to be recruited into police work to offset any built-in mistrust in the minority communities. It is at this meeting DIGNITY introduced a new sign and next slogan of our campaign, "the new Klan has no DIGNITY' Krack Kocaine Kills." and announced to the group that we were identifying other drug-infested neighborhoods to take our patrols and drug eradication efforts.

Back at DIGNITY headquarters for what quickly became a regular phenomenon. We held another afternoon press conference to announce that we would immediately precede with our efforts to stop the sale of rolling papers in the major Little Rock grocery stores. Our next visits were to Kroger and Harvest Foods. At two that afternoon DIGNITY marched into the Kroger store at 1100 E. Roosevelt one of the oldest and in one of the poorer areas in Little Rock to deliver a letter asking the chain to take the papers off its shelves. We threatened to return and take unspecified action if the chain did not contact us in seventy-two hours.

Store manager J. Andre Pendleton accepted the letter but refused to make a public comment referring media to the regional office in Memphis, Tennessee. Store staff acknowledged that they were previously warned DIGNITY was coming. There were no cigarette papers visible on the store shelves but there was a noticeable empty space in the tobacco section.

Our publicized campaign to remove paraphernalia from the shelves of the stores was making an immediate impact. The media now chasing the story to be first to report it, bombarded the Memphis Kroger regional office for comments to our demands.

Surprisingly the store promised to meet with DIGNITY to see what the national grocery chain can do to help promote our message of anti-drugs. Marnette Perry, vice-president of merchandising for approximately eleven hundred stores read a statement applauding the organization's drug eradication initiatives and offered support. "We have the chance to combine our efforts and do a lot from an informational standpoint because we have thousands of people passing through our doors every day. Perry further stated the store could display large anti-drug banners, distribute anti-drug sweatshirts, set up informational booths in all stores plus number of other ideas.

However the chain could not comply with the request that cigarette rolling papers be removed from the store shelves. The Kroger Co. in Arkansas has sold tobacco products to entire generations of customers. "The paper products are legal and have a legitimate use. Our customers decide by their purchase choice which products are available in our stores. When told of Perry's remarks neither Bill nor Dick offered a

response until they talked to store

representatives themselves and

mentioned a trip to Memphis soon.

While DIGNITY tried to get the rolling

papers off of the shelves another group

started a picket demonstration. They

supported legalizing marijuana in

respond to our anti-drug efforts. The

Arkansas chapter of NORML, the

National Organization for the Reform of

Marijuana Laws, held a counter-

demonstration beginning at Armadillo's

Hands down to the Kroger store located

one block west. NORML favors legalizing

marijuana which the group contends is

used by 20 percent of the population.

Chapter president Glen Schwarz said that

banning rolling papers would

inconvenience tobacco smokers as well

as marijuana smokers. By controlling

marijuana in a manner similar to

alcoholic beverages law enforcement

efforts could be concentrated on

dangerous chemical substances like cocaine and amphetamines.

Their demonstration drew two supporters and a news reporter.

Even Frawley probably fearing heat from the law said he did not support the NORML protesters and asked them not to hold their protest on his property.

Maintaining a pace that if you blink you might miss something, our next stop is to the office of the Arkansas Democrat where Dick was interviewed by the editorial board for an hour or so.

Afterwards, I drove him back to his hotel to refresh, regroup, make phone calls, send out letters, schedule meetings and then on to the nightly patrol which did go on as usual but at a later than normal patrol time. After Monday night's shooting we began our patrols a little later in the evening now staying after midnight since the gang activity was picking up later at night after our patrols were over. Of course now there was an increased police presence and constant eyes of the media. The group of about twenty-five tonight went out ever strong in our purpose and more invigorated from our recent activities of the week. We were now working in squads with designated responsibilities.

Through situation, circumstance or necessity I have now become Dick and his assistant Reggie Toran's personal driver. Whenever he or Reggie needed to get to or from his hotel, meetings, to the office, area churches and when they are not riding with either Bill or Rickey, I transported them. I think even though I was always present for our activities I purposefully tried to remain as incognito as possible staying out of the limelight or making attempts to draw undo attention. Quickly one of the many things I learned about Mr. Gregory was his vigilance, his attention to stay on point, his energy in spite of hardly ever seeing him drink anything other than water, that he kept and maintained himself.

He hardly ate anything that looked like food except these hard-candy looking balls that he sucked on. His fire, his compassion for people and his spiritual dedication was unmatched by anyone I had ever met before. He never disregarded or acted pretentious towards me or others. The times when it was just he and I riding in my car as we drove around Little Rock, he was attentive as I talked about growing up in Little Rock, different parts of the historical black neighborhoods and locations like Horace Mann High School, 9th Street business district, and how I felt a lot of Little Rock's city core is susceptible and in decline to crime and violence, wanting to see a change.

He asked a lot of questions about the neighborhoods we drove through.

Now he was no stranger to Arkansas or the region. Twenty-seven years ago Dick was arrested in Pine Bluff, Arkansas for trying to desegregate a restaurant on North Cedar Street.

Two years later in 1966 he participated in a protest march from south of Hernando, Mississippi where James Meredith was shot near the Tennessee state line. Another thing was his simplistic lifestyle. He did not profile himself by staying in high priced hotels nor maintained what I thought a celebrity status.

We navigated very quietly unnoticed for the most part and when he was recognized he was friendly. When we arrived at various locations in my Delta 88 he had the ability to assimilate quietly into a crowd without a lot a fanfare. It was an uncanny learning experience for me to closely observe him. At this time his spiritual dedication had him fasting for almost a month before he came to Little Rock and each night beginning that Wednesday night he was taken to Holy Temple Church of God in Christ on 14th & Pulaski Street where he conducted a prayer vigil.

Three women showed up and joined him that Friday night for a three day lock-in prayer and fast vigil.

On Saturday shortly after noon DIGNITY's next public appearance was scheduled, of all places, the county jail. But this time it was at the personal invitation of Sheriff Carol Gravette to bring our anti-drug motivational message to his captive audience in the Pulaski County Jail. We were greeted by all of the top officials in the sheriff's department and then escorted to an area where approximately sixty inmates were assembled. With Dick leading the way he used his stand-up comic appeal to break the ice before getting serious.

"Praise God we are all here today,"
"Course you all didn't have no choice."
Still proudly wearing his DIGNITY cap,
Dick rattled off stories as he strutted,
mugged and parodied members of all
races and income brackets. Dick told the
inmates that the justice system and
society as a whole is biased against poor
people and blacks but preached that faith
in God can help overcome
discrimination.

And while he preached hope he also told
them the solution to the drug problem
plaguing America was the inmates locked
inside the jails.

"We need you. And we don't need you with any attitudes. We need you with love." The prisoners roared throughout Gregory's routines, with a good portion in language not ready for television, but then he became very serious by saying,

"What you all are doing here don't satisfy God"

"This is chump time" a few of the inmates urged him on, saying "That's right" and "Tell it".

When a deputy's police radio squawked during one story, Dick said "Is that you, Lord?"

When he finished a prisoner named Adrian Tisdale told Gregory he was being tried for capital murder Tuesday and asked him, "Would you be there for me?"

Reminding Tisdale that "they stuck the death penalty on Christ," saying also he wasn't sure if he could attend the trial and urged Tisdale to pray. Many other inmates came forward to hug Dick after the talk. Sheriff staff then directed us to another location in the jail that housed about 20 juveniles aged seventeen and under.

Sine Dick was less comfortable with this age group, Bill, Jamal and Rickey did most of the talking. Only one of the youth said he knew who Dick Gregory was before Bill introduced him.

Dick told the juveniles there "ain't nothing you can learn in jail."

After about 2 hours at the jail, I drove Dick back to the church lock-in. Reggie and I completed some administrative errands. I then drove him back to the hotel. I proudly returned home to my family completing a very fruitful week of work "Walking in DIGNITY."

Saturday's patrol went on as usual with our other leaders Jamal, Ken, Johnny, Robert, the two Yusuf's and other members making sure our main focus and intent stay ever vigilant.

Sunday is a day of rest and reflection. It is when DIGNITY's activities of the previous week would be recapped by all of the local news outlets. Phone calls are coming in from national news affiliates for interviews generating their own points of view news stories. One such view was an editorial published by the Arkansas Democrat, titled Of Lights- and Rats.

Don't scoff at Dick Gregory's strategy for helping the citizens' group DIGNITY fight dope and retake local central city neighborhoods that are now controlled by drug dealers. Police officers couldn't use his approach-and probably wouldn't, even if they could. And don't write him off to publicity-hounding. We think he has proven not only his sincerity but also that his methods do disrupt illegal drug trafficking. If Gregory and his brave band of DIGNITY followers, who may even be risking their lives going out on the streets at night to challenge the drug trade, can accomplish in Little Rock what Gregory helped to achieve in Shreveport in 1989, we'll all be better off.

Shreveport's drug situation of two years ago paralleled our own.

Gregory camped for six months in a city park there and led nightly vigils on the street corners to discourage sales of illegal drugs. He and his followers triggered some 400 drug arrests during that time and their efforts broke the power of fear that the flamboyant drug dealers had imposed upon ordinary people. But Gregory's and DIGNITY's beginnings here drew the same disparaging reaction from the police that he had encountered there-as though they were meddling in a problem best left to police. Gregory said the Shreveport police had little interest in stamping out drugs until they were told, "We're going to clean up the town with or without your help." He said the same about the police attitude here, though we wouldn't go that far. But anti-drug efforts by the local police do seem to focus more on street dealers than on users. In fact the only negative comments have come from the police, as one can understand are apprehensive about the possibility that a group of unarmed civilians may succeed in halting drug traffic where the cops have failed. Instead of poor mouthing DIGNITY, police should be cooperating with them. And if the campaign succeeds the police should consider quit talking tough and go out to shine a few lights themselves.

At any rate their message has been sounded and Gregory and DIGNITY members have been going out at night to patrol the street corners where the drug pushers do their business armed only with video cameras and peaceful dialogue. As Gregory says, if you shine the light on the people who buy illegal drugs-including many white people from all walks of life who shop from their cars on those corners, they will run like rats and cockroaches. They'll run, he says, even if the video cameras have no film because they fear being seen. He's right, of course, and the flip side is that though only the users are running, the peddlers themselves can't run, for their territories have already been carved up. And when a dealer's clientele runs elsewhere, it impedes money flow, and the resultant ripple goes all the way up to those who bankroll it, putting dealers at every level of the supply network at odds with each other. When that happens the fear that has gripped the people begins to break and especially young people no longer glamorize drug dealers as the heroes of the inner cities. The false glamour of drug dealing is at the very root of not only the drug problem but also the festering sore of teen-age gangs that are most responsible for the street shootings and other violent crimes. They envy the pushers who flaunt fancy clothes and women in their expensive cars. But if Gregory and DIGNITY can scatter the drug users and disrupt their ordinary flow of business, far more will have been achieved than by the police setting snares for pushers and confiscating what they can of the dope itself. When the flow of drug money is disrupted all sorts of things begin to happen.

Born Richard Claxton Gregory, now 58 and poor in St. Louis, Missouri, escaped the rough streets of East St. Louis on a track scholarship. Finding humor in racism he developed a very successful nightclub act before the civil rights movement that earned him recognition as an activist and for a while a politician.

As an entertainer Gregory weighed 350 pounds, smoked four packs of cigarettes and drank a fifth of Scotch a day. He is married to Lillian and is father of ten children. Gregory at one time was one of the highest paid comedians in entertainment when he turned his attention to world hunger and other social ills. He began fasting to bring attention to his causes and his weight dramatically fell to 135 pounds. His activism and crusades ranged wide but his later crusades he compared to the battles of the 1960's.

To make the streets safe again for the grandmothers and grandbabies was the civil rights movement of the 1990's but comparisons vary greatly for in the civil rights movement black people were on

one side and white people on the other
for the most part. In this drug fight
everybody was on the same side. He has
been to other cities using the same
techniques to clean up one street corner
only to see the buyers and sellers run to
another. Gregory saw the potential to
introduce his anti-drug message in Little
Rock to clean out the entire city because
of the manageable size of the drug
problem and the depth of the support for
DIGNITY. Drug dealers cannot move
from one corner to another if DIGNITY
has all the corners patrolled. Gregory
claims it was fear not drugs or hoodlums
that was terrorizing American streets.
And the war against fear can be won in
Little Rock by organizing citizens and

showing them they can retake control of their neighborhoods after dark. The strategy was to finish one corner and maintain it while moving on which was something that could not be achieved in other cities like Chicago, Milwaukee, Atlanta or Pontiac. The structure and dedication of the members of DIGNITY made it a possibility in Little Rock.

Chapter Six
Prayers of the
Righteousness

DIGNITY's peaceful but unrelenting effort to rid high-crime neighborhoods of drugs and violence continued unabated. It gained momentum with the announcement on Monday July 29th that Harvest Foods Inc. had pulled all individually packaged cigarette rolling papers off the shelves of its fourteen Little Rock area grocery stores.

Harry Janson, Harvest Foods president announced, "It has always been the policy of Harvest to strive to provide the consumer with the products and services they want, It is our summation that the majority of our customers do not support the sale of individual cigarette papers." The announcement Monday followed DIGNITY"s protests last Friday against Kroger Food Store for selling the papers we claimed are used to smoke marijuana. Though not prompted directly by DIGNITY, the store's owners apparently were motivated by DIGNITY's threat of a boycott last week with K-Mart and Kroger.

One Harvest store at 14901 Cantrell Road removed its cigarette papers that Saturday. Harvest Foods' initial positive actions contrasted those of Kroger officials who balked at the request but agreed to meet with DIGNITY leaders on Tuesday in Memphis.

After the Harvest Foods announcement rumors circulated all day Monday that Kroger agreed to not sell cigarette papers without accompanying tobacco purchases. On Tuesday our president Jamal Safee-ullah along with Bill L. Walker Jr., Rickey Hicks and Dick Gregory traveled to Memphis to meet with representatives of Kroger's Delta region. The 9:30 a.m. meeting lasted about one and a half hours and was productive and amicable.

After that meeting at Kroger Company's national headquarters in Cincinnati, corporate vice president Jack Partridge sent memorandums Tuesday urging each of its eleven hundred stores nationwide to require the purchase of tobacco with cigarette papers. The recommendations went to the eleven marketing offices that oversee all regions.

The policy was implemented Tuesday morning in one hundred three stores in Arkansas, Tennessee, Kentucky, Missouri, Mississippi and Alabama. Each store in the Delta region posted signs that day acknowledging the policy change.

Returning to Little Rock the press conference was held at 3 PM.
At the news conference Bill and Dick announced DIGNITY"s successful agreement with Kroger and their new policy regarding the sale of rolling papers. We accomplished what we set out to do.
We appreciated Kroger's attitude and image to support our cause in corporate

America. We visited the store again today to thank them publicly. DIGNITY also thanked the media for delivering our anti-drug and anti-crime message quickly and firmly when Dick remarked, "The victory does not belong to us.

It belongs to the press".

Bill announced meetings had been scheduled with each chief of police of the Little Rock and North Little Rock Police Departments. The meetings were to work out any disagreements and to determine which five or six street corners in the cities were the "most drug-ridden". DIGNITY began patrolling them with a police car on hand. We also welcomed two new members who showed up during the press conference. Other than Bill and Hillary Clinton they were the first white people to join DIGNITY. North Little Rock residents Jack Morris and his daughter Tanya Gambill arrived shortly before we left to visit the store. Tanya said she and her father read about what we were doing and because they were worried for her daughter Delanie's future. "We don't want her to grow up where there's dope on every street corner," Asked if they were willing to participate in the neighborhood patrols, Jack said they were here to do whatever was asked of them. With our newest members in tow we then proceeded back

to the East Roosevelt Kroger store where
we stood outside the front window for
about 20 minutes displaying a large sign
that read, "Thank you Kroger for your
decision. You have DIGNITY.

We thank God."

We took a similar sign to Harvest Food
at 1701 S. Main Street to acknowledge
their willingness to give support to
DIGNITY's drug intervention measures.

After the successes at the beginning of
the week Wednesday's press conference
was now taking on the feel of regular
briefings of DIGNITY"s daily adventures.
We have established creditability, now
national attention plus the support of

corporate America. Dick informed the press that DIGNITY decided to patrol the five most drug plagued intersections in Little Rock and North Little Rock next week, and would be doing so "under the civil rights bill" with FBI protection. Dick said that the neighborhood marches will include anyone who wants to participate but warned the peaceful patrols are limited only to those willing to face danger. At no time will we go into an area where all the authorities haven't been briefed. The action plan will be well thought out and police will know ahead of time coordinating a police presence during the patrols. He asked everyone with video cameras in Little Rock and North Little Rock to become video marshals by filming crimes they witness. Last, Dick announced he would again lock himself in with Bishop Harold T. Walker and church members at Holy Temple Church of God in Christ without food or water from 6 p.m. Wednesday to 6 p.m. Friday as part of an ongoing fast and prayer vigil inviting the "whole town" to stop by for a rally following the fast.

Bill then announced that DIGNITY was meeting at 5 p.m. Thursday at 1321 Scott Street with the Neighborhood Coalition at Villa Mare. After the press conference again with the press following, DIGNITY's next visit that day was to the K-Mart Discount store on Asher Avenue which incidentally is directly across the street from Armadillo's Hands. DIGNITY members delivered a letter to Kmart manager Tim Jenkins asking the store chain to remove cigarette rolling papers from its shelves nationwide. Jenkins promised to forward the letter to the store's national headquarters in Troy, Michigan stating only corporate officers can make such a decision. The letter stated among other things: "We know that marijuana is a multi-billion dollar illegal business in our country. However it is mostly used with cigarette paper. Even though the use of marijuana is illegal, the selling of cigarette paper gives an aura of legitimacy to this illegal act. Whatever can be done however minute to make drug use more difficult is a plus for the future of America. The letter gave the Kmart 72 hours to respond. The letter did not specifically state what action will be taken but at other news conferences we called for a nationwide boycott of stores if they did not honor our request. Ironically the store was out of the normally stocked papers.

Dick returned to the church for the lock-in prayer vigil and the patrol that night went on as usual.

Thursday's meeting with the Neighborhood Coalition at Villa Mare was well attended by the thirteen neighborhood groups that make up the coalition. In this meeting DIGNITY urged the residents to get involved in the patrols against drugs and crimes. By being visible in large numbers in front of crack houses and on the corners claimed by the gangs as drug dealers' territories the citizens can keep the drug buyers away. Drug dealers who can't move onto one another's turf without a battle will be forced out of business. Dick said when we do this we send a ripple effect all the way back to Colombia. By drying up profits for the street-corner dealers those dealers' sources will be affected all the way up the drug pyramid. "When the neighbors see us come out there they are not the glamour boys anymore, we are." Dick was now on the 28th day of a planned 54-day fast. Today marked the third and final day he would go without food for the church fast vigil.

Always talkative Dick was now showing signs of fatigue and weakness but his determination to endure was unyielding. One suggestion he made I thought intriguing was for citizens including children from across the city each night for the next two years to gather and march for 30 minutes in designated areas. Parents should feel free to drop off their children and know they are in a safe place. Following each march which is designed to break the fear in the neighborhood, a small group of specially trained citizens will patrol the area with video cameras to thwart drug activity.

Attracting crowds on a consistent basis impresses politicians who are then forced to take action against drugs and crime. We also used this opportunity to appeal for financial support to purchase more DIGNITY T-shirts, binoculars, uniforms and video cameras to increase the visibility of DIGNITY.

I drove Dick back to the church.

Friday's new reports were that K-mart's corporate offices in Troy, Michigan haven't received DIGNITY's letter to Joe Antonini Kmart's chief executive. It asked stores not to sell cigarette rolling papers. Mary Lorenz, Kmart's public communications manager said, "We do carry them in our store. In some parts of the country many of our customers still roll their own cigarettes. But we have no idea what else people might use them for." The three Kmart stores in Pulaski County however removed them from their shelves while our protest was directly targeting them. Kmart has 2,300 stores in all 48, Canada and Puerto Rico including 17 stores in Arkansas.

It was also one week after Robert "Say' McIntosh set his deadline for Dick Gregory to get out of town. Dick was still here racking up front page headlines every day. McIntosh was not accustomed to being upstaged in a public relations war but with Dick Gregory he's more than met his match.

Everyone knows Dick is more skillful and experienced at manipulating the media. The feeling was that McIntosh was more concerned about being overshadowed by the young brash state representative Bill Walker. He managed to get his picture in the paper every time Dick Gregory did.

Gregory after all is a national celebrity who will eventually go away while Bill remains. When pressed by the media what he planned to do if Dick ignored his ultimatum, he hinted he would do something but declined to be specific, other than shooting off his mouth.

In a private meeting with Little Rock Police Chief Louie Caudell, DIGNITY leaders Rickey Hicks, Bill Walker Jr. and

Dick Gregory emphasized the need for both groups to work together to fight drugs in Little Rock and to down play tactical disagreements. Instead of police criticizing our tactics we wanted to focus on cooperation. The police department's spokesperson stated police felt used when DIGNITY staged the protest to get arrested and taken to jail at Armadillo's Hands and was critical when we first took to the streets patrolling Wright Avenue. This meeting was to make sure there is clear understanding between the two groups because what we have been doing and what we are fixing to do will not work unless we have a thorough understanding of what the police's job is and what's our job. The chief stated the department from the inception of DIGNITY has supported and will continue to do so. "We felt all along that it takes citizen involvement".

We promised in the future if we decide to go into civil disobedience mode it won't be during shift change and we don't want to play games with the police when we all have a job to do. Chief Caudell agreed that any problem that existed between the police and DIGNITY had been resolved and that police would continue to support DIGNITY and be visible during DIGNITY patrols. A short follow-up meeting outlining new initiatives was set for Monday.

DIGNITY's next objective that day was one that was intentionally unannounced publicly or to the press with them now following Bill, Rickey and Dick everywhere they go. But this meeting too will soon become a big news story. Coordinating with Reverend Hezekiah Stewart, director of the Watershed Community Development Agency on 3701 Confederate Blvd, DIGNITY convened a meeting termed the "Gang Summit" that afternoon. Selected Pulaski County officials and community leaders were invited to meet face-to-face with gang leaders and gang members from Little Rock and North Little Rock to address the increasing gang-related violence. Thirteen gang members representing

some of the larger sets including 23rd
Street Posse, the Folks, the 8-Ball Posse
and a white gang showed up for the
summit with the understanding that no
law enforcement would be present or
interfer with them commuting to and from
the meeting. There were about fifty
onlookers with a priest, a coroner, some
parents and state Rep. N.B. "Nap"
Murphy of Hamburg. Government
officials attending included an aide to
Gov. Clinton, Tracy Steele, Mayor Sharon
Priest, Vice-mayor Jim Dailey and
Pulaski County Judge Floyd G. Buddy
Villines sat at a table, hands folded while
gang members sat before them in a semi-
circle.

With DIGNITY members sitting close by, Rev. Stewart acted as the moderator of the meeting. The purpose of this encounter was for the two adversaries, so-to-speak, to meet face-to-face to see the differences and look for positive ways to bridge those differences.

This meeting was not another DIGNITY or Dick Gregory platform. This meeting was a venue to give the youth a direct voice despite their affiliation with the gangs.

The incident marked a historic but tense moment in the unusual meeting as gang members wearing masks to keep their identities secret for fear of being spotted by rival gangs and in T-shirts sitting before political leaders in business suits struggled to understand one another's problem. The few invited news photographers were forbidden to take pictures except for one and no taped recordings were allowed. The meeting began with gang members warning the politicians that a Little Rock curfew could trigger more problems than it would solve. North Little Rock recently voted for a curfew because of youth violence that would begin in three days.

One gang member explained that a Little Rock curfew would make matters worse and that an increase in gang violence could spread to more attacks on homes increasing the possibility for hurting the innocent. Mayor Priest stated that she did not foresee a curfew, "That purely would be a last resort for the city board." Another gang member noted that racism underlies many of the gangs' concerns including being harassed by police when they "hang out" in their neighborhoods.

They're angry that authorities assume black teenagers hanging out or attending public functions will always trigger violence. They say the badgering by police simply perpetuates the conflict. Another teenager said that recreation programs wouldn't stem the violence and many kids wouldn't use them. Instead saying kids prefer going to clubs. Vice-mayor Jim Dailey asked why the gang members didn't get jobs. One by one the teenagers said employers refuse to hire them because they have police records and besides the $4.25-an-hour pay is ridiculous. Naïve Jim Dailey continued saying his son was unhappy about the pay when he worked for their family business. His son by working learned a different trade and found a better paying job. One gang member retorted correctly at the poor comparison that Dailey himself comes from a family of affluence who was in business before he was born.

"Your father had it. We ain't got it."

Another explained that a teenager in his neighborhood was learning to drive and a neighbor called the police suspecting attempted car theft. "You don't get none of that in the white folks' neighborhood," he added angrily. Dailey conceded there was no way he could understand their problems. Robert McIntosh, still seeking attention arrived late, well after the meeting started. He stood up in the audience and told the gang members they themselves could do something about their problems questioning the need for violence. That prompted a gang member to reveal that kids do pay attention to their surroundings and referred to McIntosh slugging white-supremacist Ralph Forbes last year on television. "You beat that man up on TV. Why can't we do that?"

Then Dick spoke to the teenagers. He said they should work to make their neighborhoods safer. Gregory said that whites will allow blacks to kill each other as long as the shooting doesn't seep into white neighborhoods. "You've got a racist society that tolerates you until you get in their business. And then they will crush you".

The discussion was interrupted when a gang member recognized law enforcement officers were in the audience. Rev. Stewart asked the gang members to leave the room. After they left at least three police officers were identified and asked to leave. Stewart said the teenagers recognized the undercover officers. The police was asked not to attend the first gang meeting which was supposed to establish trust among the gang members and authorities.

The meeting resumed about fifteen minutes later after the officers and some of the uninvited public left. This gave Dick another opportunity to tell the gang members that they needed to respect themselves and do what black activists in the 1960's did not do. Get a share of society's wealth, perhaps by starting a business. "You all need a piece of the action, that's what a lot of us older blacks forgot to do."

Tracy Steele challenged the gang members to take advantage of this chance to influence the decision makers. Sensing it was time for this first meeting to conclude, Judge Villines recommended any future meetings with the gangs be withheld from the press because setting press ground rules were too complicated and he shook the hands of each masked gang member as they left the auditorium.

A few in the audience felt the meeting legitimized gangs and others said the whole effort was worthless because gangs could not be stopped. But two teenagers participating in Watershed's Get Ready Program which tries to rehabilitate young offenders sounded impressed. "The mayor could've sent some fuddy-duddy, the judge could have sent some fuddy-duddy. They did not have to come." With the other adding, "I ain't going to say it's a waste of time because they're trying. It's a start."

A short trip back to the hotel to freshen up I drove Dick back to Holy Temple to finish the church's lock-in prayer and fast vigil. About a hundred people attended the two-hour DIGNITY organized rally, several other speakers who were not members of DIGNITY stood to motivate the audience with speech, songs and prayers. Former drug addicts Abraham Baird and Phillip Bryant told the audience how cocaine had consumed their lives until they received help from the local drug rehab, "The GYST House" (Getting Yourself Together).

Our president Jamal Safee-ullah said, "We hope Little Rock can show the nation and the world what you can do when you get sick and tired, we have a united common cause we all must rally around." When it came time for Dick to speak he received a long standing ovation from the crowd. Dick urged the crowd to pray for the people who sell drugs, but to not fear them. "You have let them be inflated with some perverse dignity, with drugs being only a part of the movement taking place to improve life for blacks in the United States." The bigger problems are racism and sexism. Following the rally a short symbolic patrol march from the church with about sixty people walked a couple blocks to High Street.

Beverly Turner, a former cocaine user now working to help others break their addiction said the march reminded her of Dr. King's civil rights march on Washington, D.C. "It's something that's changing our world". The rally capped a busy week of work for DIGNITY.

On Sunday DIGNITY broadened its drug and gang violence eradication empowerment to North Little Rock and into the church. A rally that evening was held at the First Baptist Church on 8th &

Locust Street. First Baptist Church these days is one of the largest black churches in North Little Rock and it is also where my first religious experience began as an infant with both my grandmother and mother being long-time church members.

On this Sunday night several hundred members of the congregation and community have come out to hear what Dick has to say. The pulpit is full of all the local big-shot preachers who want to be seen in the company of someone like Dick Gregory and the event is a full service like you see in black churches with the singing, praising, praying and mini-sermons from the various speakers. Bill has become our main spokesman but the people here came out to see the celebrity Dick Gregory. When his time came Dick began by saying the black churches must play a role in any successful movement to rid the community of drugs. "There's a point where the church is going to have to stop singing the songs and start listening to them, paraphrasing the Battle Hymn of the Republic, as he was willing to die to make people holy, let us die to make people free. We need troops out there in the streets, and if you die, so what?" "You all sent your children to Kuwait and here your grandmother can't walk on the corner. Dope dealers are walking around upright like law-abiding citizens, and law-abiding citizens are cowering inside like criminals." He reminded them that churches have been a part of every important development in black history. There has never been a movement about liberation that the church wasn't a part of.

God at any moment can put his spirit in you for a mission.

He blasted President's Bush's concept "war on drugs" as a bad approach because it emphasizes violence and killing over peaceful methods and forgiveness. "What you all are doing here today is peacemaking, you've got to forgive the drug pusher. They're not animals, they're our children. And we're just out to save our children."

Dick quickly reminded the congregation that he was not going to be here long because cleaning up the Little Rock area is the responsibility of the residents by saying "We not going to give you too much time because there's too many towns saying come", and "it don't make no difference which one we do it at."

Praising the work of DIGNITY, Dick said, "When I see the brothers out there every day willing to make the ultimate sacrifice to save their community, shows me that Little Rock is an easy town to knock over if the whole community has DIGNITY."

Monday morning Bill and Dick had their follow-up meeting with Little Rock police Chief Louis Caudell to discuss and coordinate logistics for future marches into different neighborhoods in Little Rock. We wanted to expand into neighborhoods that were identified as high drug trafficking areas. They were also briefed on what drug education programs are available locally, met with members of the organized crime sections and the officer who coordinates the school D.A.R.E. program. Dick praised the meeting as "one of the most thorough and friendly he's had with any police and I'm talking about areas with black police chiefs."

It's now been a few days since the "Gang Summit" and some people are beginning to make complaints, saying the youth violence was helped when city and county officials rapped for an hour and a half with thirteen masked leaders of black gangs. Some felt it provided an aura of legitimacy for street gangs and puffed up the stature of its leaders. Others heard the threat of increased violence if the city invoked a curfew on juveniles as a way of holding officials hostage. Another unwelcome result was the risk of reinforcing the image that gang leaders are role models on their own streets which helps glamorize gangs and encourages recruitment. While there were some legitimate ideas voiced by the gangs the one thing that left little doubt about the scope of the gang problem in Little Rock, was the sheer number of represented gangs who showed up. All are valid concerns but the true fact is these leaders are the role models in their sects leading deadly successful criminal enterprises that generate the kind of money a kid won't make sacking burgers.

If you are trying to change a behavior you work with the ones who have that influence to communicate with their members about change. And hopefully with all participating there can be a change in all.

Showing proactive support to DIGNITY's very public demonstration to the sale of drug paraphernalia the Little Rock Police arrested the owner's of Armadillo's Hands and Ugly Mike

Records for selling drug devices. Facing
misdemeanor charges Joe Frawley and
James Gilliam were issued citations to
appear in court before Judge Bill Watts.
Judge Watts authorized the warrants for
the items seized by police and has
jurisdiction for misdemeanor cases
along with Judge Humphreys who
disqualified himself from the trespassing
case at Armadillo's Hands involving
DIGNITY. The charge carries a maximum
of one year in jail and up to a $1000 fine.
Their court date is August twentieth.

Tuesday DIGNITY held its daily news
conference that morning because Bill
and Dick were leaving town that day to
first visit the corporate offices of Kmart

in Troy, Michigan and then on to Atlantic City, New Jersey. They were invited to attend a joint news conference to tell the world about DIGNITY's connection with a heavyweight boxing match Friday between Riddick Bowe and Bruce Seldon in which Bowe's manager Rock Newman will voice their support for DIGNITY's war on drugs.

DIGNITY also released a list targeting fourteen new sites. Through our own surveillance and personal knowledge of these neighborhoods we determined that drug dealing regularly occurs in these locations. Announcing that we would first display by placing posters declaring these sites as "drug free zones", giving notice to the drug dealers that we have our eye on you and we want you to stop selling drugs here. The announcement is a way of giving clear notice to everyone when we are coming and that they should abandon those sites. Most are intersections where major drug dealing occurs and where our patrols will begin. The aim as always is to discourage prospective customers from entering the drug dealers' territories. If that doesn't work then we will introduce the video cameras. Chief Caudell when contacted by the press agreed that the locations DIGNITY selected were fairly accurate areas with the worst drug problems but added that his feeling is that when you attack a small area, you drive away dealers but with no permanent change they eventually come back. He did say that his recent meeting with DIGNITY has convinced him that the group may succeed because its plan includes getting neighborhood residents to help in retaking streets from drug traffickers.

The fourteen sites identified are 33rd & Pulaski, 26th & Maple St, East 6th & Harrington, Valley Drive, Frazier Pike, 15th & Oak, 23rd & Gaines/State Streets, 29th & Wolfe, 26th & Battery, 26th & Arch, 33rd & Boyd, 12th & Woodrow, 21st & Bragg and I Street in Dixie Addition, North Little Rock.

The foot patrols with about ten members will continue nights along Wright Avenue and High Street because we will always maintain a presence in the area we began and now with increased police presence we patrol in shifts. We also announced that only people recommended by DIGNITY members will be allowed to patrol with us to prevent someone from masquerading as patrollers to further their own causes or to tarnish DIGNITY's quickly growing credibility and reputation. Playing it by ear but coordinating with police so that we do not interfere with any undercover operations we will randomly select up to three sites per night to patrol staying in the targeted areas up to six months.

Dick utilizing his influence as an icon and civil rights activist took his anti-drug message to the national airwaves Friday with a five-minute interview on CNN's "Sonya Live" interview show. Emphasizing his recent work with DIGNITY Gregory talked about our efforts to force stores from selling rolling papers which gives the aura of legitimacy to those who use them to roll marijuana cigarettes. Dick acknowledged both Kroger and Harvest Foods as setting the pattern for corporate America to get involved. Involving corporate America in the drug war is essential.

Dick also urged people in communities nationwide to organize like we have in

Little Rock, praising state Rep. Bill Walker and DIGNITY.

Later that night members of DIGNITY were again placed in the national spotlight at the Riddick Bowe vs. Bruce Seldon heavyweight boxing match. The fight was shown across the United States on pay-per-view cable. As they entered the arena Bowe's corner men and manager wore DIGNITY hats with Dick, Bill and Rickey following close behind Bowe's manager as they walked to the ring. The spotlight went out quickly however when Bowe ended the fight with a technical knockout in the first round.

About fifteen of us gathered at the home of DIGNITY members Eric Payne and

Bryon Shells to watch the fight. We all cheered loudly when we saw Bill and Rickey along with Dick proudly representing and introducing to the nation our organization which was mentioned several times by the ring announcers. After the fight Brock Newman, Bowe's manager stated Bowe wanted to help the group by coming to Little Rock and later sent a telegram thanking the group for the work it is doing and for being in his corner.

After almost three weeks of intense public interaction around the city of Little Rock and garnering DIGNITY national attention to our fight against drug abuse and gang violence, Dick

Gregory would not return to Little Rock, but his personal assistant Reggie Toran would remain and coordinate with us through him for another month.

We continued our prayers for direction and God provided that to us.

It is back on us to continue the work without the limelight but we are still dedicated to continue to make significant changes for our children in Little Rock.

The media feeding frenzy now over DIGNITY without Dick Gregory at the helm has left opportunity for the people who live in and around the Wright Avenue and High Street area. A chance to be interviewed by the still remaining national and local press to give their assessments on the serenity and safety of their neighborhood by the number of gunshots heard in the night and the number of teens loitering in the parking lots. To one resident Diane Fox who lives in the Village Square apartments the patrols appear to be working. Fox said, "It's a lot quieter than it used to be." "You know someone's over there watching," added James Hendrix, sitting a couple of steps up from Fox. They pointed to the carwash across the street where several people were doing what's usually done at a carwash, washing their cars. The teens still hang out but now they seem to be leaving their pistols home. "Since "DIGNITY has been walking

around, the crowd is not as bad," said
Yvonne Redout another apartment
resident. "They used to shoot on
Saturday and Sunday nights, but they
don't do that anymore. They just hang
out, but no shooting." A few blocks down
the street Eugene "Al-Right" Andrews
said, "The most important thing about
DIGNITY is not that they curb drug
abuse, but they force criminals off the
street, even out of the neighborhood.
People are aware that they're being seen,
that the eyes are on what they are doing,"
adding "I'd be a plumb idiot to say
they're stopping drugs but I think some
people have cleaned up." Andrews
continuing, "This used to be a bad spot.
Six months ago you could not sit out on

your front porch because of all the
people out there drinking and selling
drugs. And DIGNITY members don't just
stroll, keeping to themselves. They get
on your nerves. People say, Here come
these pests, let's chill out.' They worry
people to the point where they just stay
out of their way."

Another result of our notoriety was the
numbers of calls and letters coming in
from all over the state asking how others
can set up anti-crime marches and
patrols. Interested parties from Pine
Bluff, Fayetteville, Ashdown and Lonoke
contacted the headquarters seeking
information. All were invited to come to
Little Rock to observe the neighborhood

marches in the next coming weeks and to learn how to conduct the marches and patrols. After announcing the new sites where DIGNITY would be patrolling, we also mentioned that we have streamlined our patrols so when we go into the more dangerous areas the video cameras would be utilized as a deterrent to crime.

The purpose behind the marches was to show strong community alliance against drugs and crime and to capture the attention of politicians who can push for crime fighting legislation. It was not a black movement; it's everybody's movement to reclaim their neighborhoods block by block to force the drug dealers from our street corners, neighborhoods, Little Rock and finally out of the state.

The contagious enthusiasm by the community for DIGNITY makes our cause more effective but like any war being waged; the war on crime needs financial backing so fundraising must become a part of this process.

As news traveled around the country of DIGNITY's drug fighting crusade, it inspired Dallas activist Imam Yahya Abdullah founder of African-American Men Against Narcotics (AAMAN) to travel to Little Rock to patrol with us. Started three years previous to fight drugs and crime in south Dallas, his group has served as the model for at least six citizens' groups that patrol Dallas neighborhoods regularly. He is here to offer his support to DIGNITY but his philosophy about what to do with major drug dealers, murderers and rapists was extreme. He believed if proven guilty beyond a shadow of a doubt the offender should be publicly executed. "Strict laws in society are a mercy to society and loose laws are a punishment," Abdullah adding, he believes imprisoning people for life is an unjustified burden on taxpayers.

Not giving any direct credit to DIGNITY on Tuesday, August 13th K-mart corporate officials in Troy, Michigan released a letter sent by facsimile to the press saying the company plans to "instruct all our tobacco product distributors to remove cigarette papers from our stores in the near future." The letter dated August 8th, signed by Dick Benoit, buyer for the corporation and addressed to State Rep. Bill Walker, Rev. Rickey Hicks and Dick Gregory says in the letter that K-mart has been considering for some time discontinuing the sale of cigarette papers due to lack of consumer demand. Benoit adds; "While we are doing this for business reasons, if it makes illegal drug use more difficult, so much the better." The letter also states the company appreciates DIGNITY sharing their concerns. At the encouragement of DIGNITY three national store chains representing over four thousand stores have now agreed to stop selling rolling papers.

"WARNING: This area declared drug FREE," read the signs DIGNITY posted by Rickey and I on utility poles in two newly targeted Little Rock neighborhoods. The large adhesive backed posters were distributed by us in a three-block area around the intersections of 23rd and Arch Street and 25th and Maple Street. Also we handed out colorful fliers door-to-door and to motorists. The fliers were a warning to the community that in forty-eight hours DIGNITY will return to this neighborhood and we asked the residents to join us.

After saturating the neighborhoods with our message, Bill announced at the news conference that DIGNITY will begin patrolling those two new areas with video cameras Friday night. The areas were added to the list of fourteen that was released on the 6th.

Some residents near 23rd and Arch who called themselves a "bunch of alcoholics" who didn't want their nightly drinking disturbed denied there was any illicit drug use but police reports revealed that shots are fired frequently in the area and from our own personal knowledge of the neighborhood we knew those comments to be only partially true.

Susan Boon, president of the Downtown Neighborhood Association who lives nearby says drugs are a problem but she believes its people who don't live here but those who frequent the nearby five liquor stores.

Chanting anti-drug slogans twenty-five DIGNITY members again marched in two single-file lines up and down Little Rock streets Friday night as we expanded our anti-crime campaign into the two new areas. I recommended the first stop. It was a very busy crack house on 25th & Oak Street. The corner lot house provided easy parking for the drug buyers to come and exit quickly. But late at night when the crack was being smoked there would be cars parked all around the three block area. There also were three liquor stores in close proximity for people to also park and walk to and from the crack house. What made this location personal and deadly real for me was that I had family members living just two houses away and two of my childhood friends of many years were living directly across the street on the opposite corners also raising their children. My in-laws had two teenage girls and they complained of the fear they had from strange looking people they did not know walking through the alley behind his house or when his children walk in the neighborhood. The house is also a block from Garland

Elementary School. We came a few days earlier and posted our drug free warning signs all around the area. In retaliation some idiots did a drive-by shooting at their house while they were inside. Fortunately thank God, no one was injured but the house had two bullet holes in it. This location was not one of the main target sites we initially chose but I went to the group requesting that we give immediate attention to that location and that we warn the police. All were in agreement. For two hours DIGNITY group members dressed in our now trademark black, armed with walkie-talkies, megaphones, flashlights and video cameras went into full combat mode. We wanted to make sure they knew who we were and why we are there. We marched up the streets with determined efficiency looking the part of a military unit and stood boldly in front of the crack house chanting, "Down with dope, Up with hope," and "Down with drugs, Up with love."

The movement was so effective that young children look out of their doors and chorus our chants, "Who are we?" "DIGNITY!" They also beg us to get drugs out of their neighborhood. A man who lives in the neighborhood named Marcus identified the house as a crack-house. There were five cars parked when we arrived. He said that there would be more but there are at least five cars there always. Someone peeped out of the back window, stared briefly at us but quickly closed the curtains. A lady walking by said, "Ya'll doing it, ain't ya?" Marcus identified her as a crack user.

We then moved on to 23rd and Gaines streets and repeated the process. There is another house identified as a crack house by Bill. Bill lives in a house on Gaines Street in the Quapaw Quarters just mere blocks away. After making our stand at this location for about an hour we began marching around the block of that location greeting and meeting anyone outside in their yards or on their front porches. Jim Brainaird who lives in one of the houses we passed joined the march for a while. Brainaird said he would "march anytime they want me to," "the drug problem in this community is very bad and he hopes that DIGNITY's efforts would do something to eliminate the problem."

At one point we heard the sound of glass breaking behind us which turned out to be two youth throwing beer bottles in our direction as they ran away. A car even swerved toward us narrowly missing three members as it quickly sped away. The police always close by now gave quick pursuit. I don't know if they were arrested or not. Despite this we still continued on before returning back to finish that night of patrolling our familiar turf on Wright Avenue. Later after assessing the evening we felt confident we could have the same effect that we had on Wright Avenue but decided we may break into smaller groups to hit certain areas simultaneously and to not announce publicly ahead of time where we will be as we did on the first two patrol sites. Sometime after midnight the narcotics unit served a search warrant on the house on Oak Street, seizing a small quantity of crack cocaine and made two arrests. Others who lived there but not there when police first arrived were later identified as having outstanding warrants.

DIGNITY was out patrolling again the next night holding steadfast to our mission—"to stop the spread of drugs in our neighborhoods." As we were ending our Saturday night activities on Arch Street a metallic blue Nissan King Cab truck appeared on Gaines Streets. Shortly after the driver turned the corner, three shots rang out. One of the DIGNITY trail cars equipped with a mobile phone added for these special patrols sped after the truck. After a two minute chase the truck was spotted five blocks away at 22nd and Ringo streets. Police were nearby and their speedy action lead to the arrest of two men. Fortunately, no one was hurt.

In what is called an unsuccessful attempt to intimidate DIGNITY into staying off the streets two men were charged with aggravated assault for firing at the DIGNITY patrol. Arrested were Tyrone Layne, 27, and Malous Griffin Jr. and police recovered a .38 caliber revolver with three rounds spent from the truck. A police spokesman said that police supported DIGNITY's goals but added that police expected that eventually someone would use violence to try to stop the patrols. "Really you have to understand that they're going in places where shooting goes on all the time, especially when they're out there trying to stomp down something some people would like them to leave alone."

Bill responded by saying, "One of the things we understood when we got into this is that they would try to resist. We basically cut-off drug business in that area, at least when we were there." We can only say that this is our community and we have more of a right to live our lives in our community than you have to abuse us. People get terrorized and harassed every day." Reggie Toran said he sees the response to the patrols as a sign that area drug dealers are beginning to feel DIGNITY's presence. "The drug dealers realized that the DIGNITY patrols heightened the awareness of people and a stand has been taken against the street sale of drugs, they are trying to intimidate and cut off that action so they can control the streets again." We also announced that we are increasing the patrols but did not inform that we will videotape the more suspicious or threatening vehicles and their license plates. We also added an extra trail car and continued to communicate with the police department.

But mostly we will be more prayerful for peaceful solutions in our mission.

Unrelated to the incident that happened that night, as Rickey was leaving the police station after filing reports of the shooting his personal vehicle collided with another vehicle that ran a red light causing his Blazer to flip over. He was taken by ambulance to Baptist Medical

Center's emergency room where he was treated for back strain and released.

For the next three weeks DIGNITY intensified our patrols around the neighborhood of 23rd and Arch Streets. Some nights our patrol would extend to Roosevelt Road which bordered another gang's territory. On randomly picked nights and at different times we thoroughly interrupted a lot of drug business because wherever we go the police are not far behind and in some cases pre-warned and already posted.

The house on 25th Street is now closed down because of its notoriety from the papers and from being identified on frequent televised news reports. We expanded the patrols into two more areas and in each area local residents wanting their neighborhoods cleaned up would come out and join the patrols. In every neighborhood we went into those who were receptive were counseled into being more proactive and to contact their city leaders letting them know that they want to help in some way. DIGNITY is now engaged in daily meetings with city staff and studying ways to cooperatively work together because we realize the problem is way too big for twenty-five weary middle-age men with limited cash resources. City leaders back in the spring looking for similar solutions to many problems that needed addressing in Little Rock conducted a community

wide goal setting and strategic visioning
process. Carried out through volunteers
utilizing citizens from all parts of the
community crossing geographic,
economic and racial lines FUTURE-Little
Rock Steering Committee was formed. It
would be a collaborative visioning
approach in problem solving by
harnessing the collective creative
energies and talents of our community.
This is why when it formed as an
organization we had such a diverse
mixture of professional talents and skills
that added with the infusion of Dick
Gregory's celebrity, knowledge and
ability to attract attention, DIGNITY is
now a very visual presence in the
community with credibility, respect and a

listened to voice. It is within these settings where I can best mobilize my skills and talents on behalf of DIGNITY by representing the organization as its executive director and primary administrator. I joined Future-Little Rock Task Force.

The committees I worked on were Public Safety and Security co-chaired by Jim Dailey and Robert Johnston and the Community and Racial Diversity co-chaired by Pat McGraw and Jim Lynch.

The public schools are open and DIGNITY is getting many requests to visit the schools to share our anti-drug, anti-gang prevention messages.

Our gaining notoriety has increased our responsibilities significantly to the point we are reassessing, where to place our best efforts for efficiency.

Reginald Toran, Dick's assistant has now left Little Rock and reports are that Dick is now in Africa.

It's now almost seven weeks since our confrontation with Joe Frawley, owner of Armadillos Hands. Pleading not guilty, his trial on misdemeanor charges of selling drug paraphernalia is held before Judge Bill Watts. Frawley testified during the hour long trial that the devices have legitimate uses and that he was unaware they could be use to ingest or weigh illegal drugs. "I don't know what's legal.

We were selling nothing but tobacco
pipes. If I can't sell tobacco pipes, they
need to close everybody in this town that
sells pipes." Frawley even insisted that
the pipes could be used among other
things such as plumbing. Seven devices
that narcotics officers bought or
confiscated from a display case in the
store were presented as evidence during
the trial. Narcotics officers testified that
the short open-ended stone pipes and
threaded cylindrical metal pipes of
varying lengths combined with
mouthpieces are used to smoke
marijuana and crack cocaine.
Prosecuting Attorney, Mark Stodola
presented the state's case said that
Frawley's testimony was totally

unbelievable and accused Frawley of "lying through his teeth." Even Judge Watts noted that he occasionally repairs plumbing on his rental properties. "I would not plumb a sink with anything that was presented on his bench. There's not a tobacco shop worth its salt that sells plumbing fixtures." Judge Watts found him guilty of selling drug devices, fined him $750 and sentenced him to six months in jail, then warned him to remove the items completely from his store or face a second arrest and harsher penalties. The judge ordered police to return to the store to see if the illegal items were still being sold and if so, to arrest Frawley on a second offense which would be a felony, and noting that

Frawley had been a plaintiff in a 1984 federal lawsuit challenging the state's drug paraphernalia law as unconstitutionally vague. A U.S. district judge subsequently ruled the law was constitutional and the decision was upheld by the 8th U.S. Circuit Court of Appeals in St. Louis when he appealed. Though it was not DIGNITY's attempt to put anyone in jail even so with Frawley's conviction the message put other head shop owners on notice that selling such drug devices in Little Rock will not be tolerated anymore. Our victory of putting those on notice who sell drug paraphernalia that the law was now focusing on removing these devices from the shelves of stores who profit legitimately off of drug use was short lived.

That evening just prior to us going on patrol a shooting occurred in the DIGNITY patrolled area of 23rd Street about half a block from Gaines Street, John Scott age 15 was shot to death about 7:30 PM.

He was shot once in the left chest when about six or seven shots were fired from a semiautomatic handgun police later identified as a 9mm pistol. Witnesses interviewed at the scene said it appeared that at least three people including Scott were standing on the north side of 23rd Street near the alley when shots came from a gray or green Ford Grenada with tinted windows. Because of the tint it could not be determined how many people were in the vehicle when the shots were fired. Nicknamed "Yellow Boy", Scott did not live in the neighborhood but evidently was known to hang out there. Mortally wounded he died in the front yard of Susan Boone, president of the Downtown Neighborhood Association who lives at 23rd and Gaines St. She was about 20 feet from her husband who happened to be mowing his grass. Police quickly identified and arrested Ronald Eugene Jones for killing Scott. Jones 35, a career criminal was gunning for someone else who used Scott as a shield when he shot and killed Scott. Arrested Friday on murder charges, Jones through a local bondsman paid $10,000 and was mistakenly released on Saturday by a civilian jailer despite a $100,000 bond and a police computer warning identifying Jones as an "escape risk" was still at-large.

In actuality Jones should not have even been on the streets to commit this crime. He was arrested in July on two counts of possession of controlled substances cocaine and Dilaudid. Already on parole from 1983 drug, burglary and theft convictions a parole revocation hearing was set but delayed at the request of Sgt. Jay Campbell a narcotic detective with the sheriff's office and Sgt. Mike Sylvester narcotics supervisor at the Little Rock

police department. In fact it was
Campbell who found Jones after being
informed of the slaying and took him to
the police Department for questioning
which led to the murder charges.
Campbell denied playing any part in
Jones' release following the murder
charge filing while the Little Rock police
claimed it was human error for the
release. As more news trickled out about
Jones it was revealed that at the time of
the shooting he was working for Little
Rock police and Pulaski County Sheriff's
office as a drug informant with
international drug connections and is
now suspected by authorities to be
heading to Mexico. Blasting the police
Judge Marion Humphries who Saturday

morning set the bond later said he wished police had informed him of the "escape risk warning" because he would have set the bond at one million dollars. Humphrey said police should re-evaluate their methods of allowing middle and high-level drug dealers to go free, only to bring in lower level drug dealers or confiscations of minuscule amount of drugs. "I never see the big fish, If these people are doing so much for the police, their work must bear fruit. The informant ought to lead the police to something or the police should stop giving them breaks."

An unrelated twist to this story is that I knew Ronnie as a child growing up in Little Rock. In fact his parents and other siblings lived in the house that was directly behind our house on the same block separated only by an alley. His older brothers and I played sport games and hung out plus being neighbors we saw each other all the time.

When Ronnie killed this child I did not realize it at the time that it was him. I am thirty-eight and Ronnie is thirty and we had not been in either one's company in many years so I was not aware of his extensive criminal lifestyle and seven year prison record. Paroled a year earlier when Ronnie was arrested in July he was carrying six-thousand dollars in cash, a large quantity of cocaine and a gun.

The young man John Eric Scott was born May 5, 1976 in Little Rock. He died September 12, 1991 violently at the age of fifteen on the streets of Little Rock. John's funeral was held Wednesday, September 18th at Greater Second Baptist Church becoming a now all too familiar scene at many of Little Rock's churches while making the funeral homes the most prosperous black businesses in town. To somewhat temper the harsh feelings of Ronnie still being on the loose on the very day John Scott was buried, police arrested a second man involved in killing

Scott. Michael Anthony Burel was charged with first-degree murder. Scott's death is the second homicide in the 2300 block of Gaines since July. Two teenagers ages 16 and 17 were charged with first degree murder in the drug-related shooting of Monte Ray Rogers, 33.

As our presence in the Arch Street area intensified, incidents of criminal behavior are also on the rise. During one of our recent meetings with city manager Tom Dalton, he suggested to begin earnestly looking for a building to permanently house the DIGNITY organization that could be funded through the city's "Fighting Back" grant program.

Emboldened by DIGNITY's daily patrols on the streets, the city wanted to make a visible statement giving financial and technical support to us. Many of the people that lived in the violence zones frustrated by the violence immediately began placing white crosses in their front yards in memory of Scott. They gathered into a group of about fifty then took their frustrations and disgust to city hall. They blamed the city, in part, for John Scott's death in what they described as the city's ongoing unresponsiveness to problems of violence, drugs and deteriorated housing in their neighborhoods. They also demanded an explanation from city board members why Ronald Jones was mistakenly released from jail Saturday. Susan Boone whose husband went to John's aid after the shooting, said, "This kid was dead in our yard..... I felt guilt, and I hope everybody in this room feels guilty because we could have prevented this." She reminded the board that the group came to them in May as a neighborhood association asking for help with neighborhood crime and deteriorating properties. She and others said it took this boy's death and DIGNITY's presence for the city to finally respond with some additional street lighting and increased police surveillance. DIGNITY also in numbers attended the city board meeting. State Rep. Bill Walker said there was something wrong with a system in which a man who has served prison time is charged with murder and then set free.

He then invited board members to join our patrols in the neighborhoods and asked for a review of the police narcotics division. Walker added that if the city didn't take more aggressive action to stop drugs and violence, "We're going to have a war zone like you've never seen."

A former member of the Planning Commission and local resident Rose Collins stated she was tired of just shaking her head and wringing her hands. "It's time to take action" she demanded of city leaders. Anxious and responding to citizens demands to rid crime, city officials that night announced that a miniature city hall, the first of five expected to eventually be established across the city will be staffed by at least one police officer. Two housing staff and a member of the community group DIGNITY would soon be housed at a location identified at 2220 Arch Street. The previous week DIGNITY members met with Tim Polk, director of Neighborhoods and Planning to discuss the idea of establishing Neighborhood Service Centers to allow the residents to become stakeholders within their own neighborhoods with direct support of the city and services.

One of the things DIGNITY discussed as a group was when we are identified for individual leadership roles in the community, did we as individuals want to take up those roles or did we want instead the organization's mission to serve as the role model for neighborhoods. Thus empowering the people themselves to become the primary stakeholders as we try to return back into our already established lives and careers. Plus we had other neighborhoods identified that we were committed to and needed our attention. I personally wanted to continue to work developing youth prevention and intervention programs throughout the city as my way of continuing to make a difference.

By Wednesday a well motivated city had secured the small 1600 square foot one-story building located on Arch Street. Plans include reshaping the interior into eight offices, a reception area, meeting room to accommodate forty people with toilet facilities. The Downtown Neighborhood Association and Little Rock's "Fighting Back" Neighborhood Alert program also will place staff in the site. With our main objective obtained for that neighborhood and the knowledge that the city was now motivated to continue to work with us to obtain positive results for its citizens in other areas, DIGNITY declined the city's offer to accept office space. When the new alert center opened in three weeks but offered instead to continue to work with neighborhoods throughout the city whenever needed. We decided we wanted to maintain our autonomy and not be seen or bound by governmental restrictions in case we decided to commit other acts of civil disobedience. Our independence is very important to us because we are now in communications with other communities and out of state organizations. Also we are secretly communicating with the two main rival gangs on reducing the violence in certain parts of town. We are attempting to mediate the continuing violence in well known "killing zones" in the city, particularly around Centennial Park where many drive-by shootings and killings had occurred.

Chapter Seven
Incredible Things

As winter began to bring colder temperatures our efforts to maintain the patrols slowed dramatically mainly because fewer people are on the streets. Our focus was now more into developing the organization DIGNITY into a viable sustaining entity in the city. We began looking into how we could do more activities through public relations and partnership building.

More and more community leaders from various parts of the city were now being vocal and proactive. Our immediate need was to find a more suitable location for our office. We still had some money left from the $15,000 governor Clinton gave us giving us the ability to set up an office. The location we found was the old Roc-Ark Water Company building on the corner of 23rd and Pulaski Street about five blocks south of Wright Avenue. The water company had closed years ago and the building sat virtually un-used. The building was sound and secure. It even had natural spring water still flowing inside the building. The site was ideal because in front was a dead-end street facing High Street a block away to the west. It was a beige colored-brick structure with few windows to gain entry and it had a garage for a large truck while protected by a ten foot barb-wired fence. It would become our own little fortress to store and protect our equipment. We also started looking into another idea we talked about and mentioned to the press as another way to increase our patrols and be secure. We wanted something that could also be used as a public relations tool.

We decided to look into the purchase of an armored truck used by Brinks and Wells Fargo to transport money.

Contacting a local security transporting company we located an old truck, one no longer in service at a nearby salvage yard. We purchased the armored truck after negotiating a reasonable price after finding out that the vehicle could be driven with some repairs and tires. With a new coat of black paint with the DIGNITY name and logo, a tune-up and new battery we were able to get it inspected, insured and licensed.

We worked hard to have it ready to drive in the 1992 Martin Luther King Jr. parade and did introduce it to the community. Enlisting those who had marched in the patrols to joins us, when the day came the DIGNITY truck made a dramatic immediate impact with the people as we carried our signs, shouted our chants of

"Up with Hope", "Down with Dope",
passed out literature about domestic
violence, black-on-black crime, gave out
candy, t-shirts and prevention stickers to
the children. We recruited a large group
of approximately eighty people along
with about twenty nice expensive cars
with signs loaned by two local auto
dealerships to show support for DIGNITY
and its message against drugs and
violence. The MLK parade campaign was
a public relations success on many
levels because there were new
discussions on how we were expanding
our crusade against the violence
visually. With the armored truck we
showed that we were ready to go into any

neighborhood despite its reputation to attack drugs and violence.

The truck though was used in many positive public relations activities at the local schools and other events where we continued to bring our message of hope. Now with a new home for the organization, an armored truck for added visibility and protection we began putting in place the administrative structure so that we could operate as a viable organization. We established written purposes, goals and an agenda in which to operate and I was officially tagged as executive director to represent DIGNITY.

I felt this to be a natural choice since I was the only one who had the experience working extensively and professionally for years with young people.

As we approached Easter 1992 our first year as a community action group we reflected back on how much had been accomplished in those twelve short but extremely eventful months. We went from being a collection of individuals with a sole purpose to save lives on the blocks where we grew up from the gangs and violence to a spiritual band of men with a vision into an organization that drew worldwide attention. It drew a national civil rights icon, a governor, a professional boxer, judges, activists from

other communities, and we made
substantial differences in changing the
attitudes of the people of Little Rock. We
even boldly ventured into the national
corporate world to expose how millions
of dollars were being made off the illegal
drug trade through the sale of
paraphernalia. Now in the light the
corporations saw the benefit of agreeing
to our demands to show they did not
support drug use.

The work of the Little Rock Task Force
for the Prevention of Youth Violence is
also progressing with more and more
stakeholders and youth services
providers coming to the table. The buzz
words now are network and collaborate.

For years many nonprofit organizations, schools and juvenile systems that sought grant funding for their programs were on a competitive basis with everyone fighting for the same dollars. This meant everyone kept ideas for their programs close to their vest like guarded secrets. The task force members also felt that we should focus on comprehensive strategies for all youth not just those associated with gangs and violence.

Facilitated by DIGNITY, the city of Little Rock and the nonprofit group New Future for Little Rock Youth, invitations were sent out to all known youth organizations, groups and religious ministries for the first city-wide meeting held that spring. Thirty-three attendees with a common goal met and began developing a strategic plan for a "Safe Summer in 1992" and established working committees. City Manager Tom Dalton served as our first chairman in this effort. That group of thirty-three quickly grew to about one hundred youth serving professionals, city and county government, law enforcement, neighborhood associations, churches, businesses, schools, parents and most importantly our youth.

The committees established were Public Awareness, Community Resources Development, Youth Initiative Project/Prevention, Youth Advisory

Committee, Finance, Public Policy,
Program Review and Special Events.

I volunteered and served as the chairman
of the Youth Initiative Project or YIP as it
became known and co-chaired the Youth
Advisory Committee. The first and most
ambitious effort of the task force was
"Operation Safe Summer" to work hard to
drastically lower the number of teen
deaths associated with violence during
the hot summer months in Little Rock.
Taking the leadership role in this
initiative my committee the Youth
Initiative Project, a model youth program
was created to engage youth in their own
neighborhoods and work to reduce

youth violence, crime, gang activity, school failure and unemployment.

Our message was through empowerment, enrichment and recruitment. We would provide productive idea alternatives to gangs and violence. Through funding provided by the city and grants that summer nine neighborhood YIP sites were identified and started throughout the city in the neighborhoods identified as most needed. To introduce the YIP program and to begin "Operation Safe Summer" we held another event "Power Jam Friday". This was a task force sponsored event held at the end of the school year.

Safely transported by Little Rock school buses over a thousand youth were invited and attended an afternoon of youth-focused workshops and engaged in recreational activities on the historic campus of Central High School. Many naysayers were concerned that with so many youth coming together from different neighborhoods in the city that there would be violence and bloodshed. YIP worked vigorously to get the word out and educate the youth that any acts of violence, throwing gang signs or any indication of gang identification would be cause for immediate removal by the police. But because of the hard work of the youth there was not even one incident of inappropriate behavior reported and all the youth appeared to enjoy the activity.

We marketed the workshops as the most important educational components because some of them would be conducted by college and high school students, their own peers.

The Youth Advisory Council along with the task force committee provided the topics for the workshops to keep them interesting and thought provoking. The Youth Advisory Council provided the proactive voice for the youth of Little Rock by working closely with government, business and community leaders to promote effective drug prevention and peaceful alternatives to youth violence.

When we introduced the idea for the council we were amazed by the young talent that began showing up and wanting to offer ideas to engage the youth.

One way which was sponsored immediately to get the youth involved was the Phat Lip! Youth Talk Radio show that aired on Saturdays from eleven to noon on KABF 88.3 FM, a hundred thousand watt station that reached not only all of Little Rock but also outside the state of Arkansas.

As a note we used the term Phat before Russell Simmons, Baby Phat and all of the other Phat references that began showing up after our radio show first aired. The radio show explored many youth issues and gave youth an interactive vocal public access. Youth Advisory Council members hosted the show and were part of a working news team and editorial group that gathered news and information that interest youth and reported on it. Striving to be the main voice of youth in the city the council welcomed all ethnic groups that make up our community because it was through cultural exchanges that all youth issues were explored, highlighted, addressed and shared.

To show the youth the task force valued their input, council members attended their meetings at city hall held in the conference room of the Fighting Back program. They formed committees to work on various points of interest and the council president gave periodic updates at the city director's meetings.

The next couple of years Power Jam Friday moved and was held on the campus of the University of Arkansas at Little Rock. The event focused on summer safety and gave young people who might not otherwise have the opportunity a chance to experience the atmosphere of a college campus and see an option for the future.

Another event sponsored by DIGNITY to get the Little Rock Police involved was the "Bridging the Gap Basketball Game" played between YIP participants and officers. The purpose was to diffuse stereotypes and tensions between the two groups and to introduce the community policing programs now in the neighborhood alert centers. This would not have happened if not for the special youth who decided they wanted to make a difference in their neighborhood and city.

Rochelle Webb was the first president of the Youth Advisory Council.

She was a talented young woman who displayed special leadership and courage despite the fact that basically everyone in her household was heavily involved in drugs and crime which she witnessed on a daily basis. Her youthful voice though small, was a voice that was heard by all and when she spoke it was with clarity and of purpose. There were other youth involved that made significant contributions to this effort and strategy but Rochelle in my opinion deserved this special notation. The city also hired Donnie Rayford as the Youth Services Coordinator to be the direct link to the city for all task force for youth activities. Donnie and I would work on several projects over the next three years.

It also became apparent that as the various coalitions were forming into proactive community partnerships the role of DIGNITY in the community was also changing and diminishing with our primary objectives being met. Now that the city and its leadership were focusing on the problems of gang violence and drug abuse and with the support of the community, the schools, government and the people, our role as the provocateur was becoming no longer necessary.

I decided since I had the experience and education I would continue in my role as a facilitator for the organization by attending meetings and participating in panel discussions on behalf of DIGNITY.

I also served on Attorney General Winston Bryant's statewide Gang Task Force he convened because statistical data now showed Little Rock was now ranked fifth as the most dangerous city in the United States.

In 1993 the Arkansas General Assembly created the state's Dr. Martin Luther King Commission and from that beginning the Arkansas Youth Assembly was created to broaden the voice of youth and to identify potential youth leaders from all over the state.

1993 was also the year I met Ken Richardson when he was hired by New Futures for Little Rock Youth as the coordinator of the Youth Initiative Project. I too had applied for the position but when I met Ken I knew they made the right selection. I embraced this younger brother as a protégé' and immediately requested he co-chair the YIP committee with me and eventually he became the chairman. That year we held the second Bridging the Gap Basketball Game, the youth won this year. Another event was the "Rainbow of Love" bowling tournament started and co-sponsored by the Civitan Club of Little Rock. Up to two hundred at-risk-youth participated with local youth-serving organizations which competed as members of bowling teams. Youth Sports Night began also as an annual event to reward at-risk-youth participating in our safe summer programs. The privately owned Little Rock Athletic Club opened its doors to one hundred youth for a night of fun which included swimming, racquetball, aerobics and dinner donated by other local civic organizations.

Power Jam Friday reached new heights when it was held at the University of Arkansas at Little Rock campus. The school had recently built a new swimming complex, gymnasium and other major renovations offering an ideal location to bring in over three thousand students from all over the city for educational workshops, fun, food, and a day to be a kid without fear of retaliation.

The next year the event was held at Macarthur Park which drew over five thousand youth and adults. Each year that we coordinated the events, it happened without incident or anyone ever being attacked or harmed.

In 1994 Little Rock voters passed the half-cent sales tax initiative recommended by the Little Rock Task Force visioning statement to invest these resources in its citizens by providing jobs, economic opportunities, education, a healthful environment and a safe attractive place to live.

The tax stipulated that for every dollar spent on enforcement an equal amount must be spent on prevention, intervention and treatment services for substance abuse and youth violence. The first year the tax generated over three million dollars. With these under-forecasted significant revenue it allowed the city to take over the administration and funding of many Fighting Back programs.

No longer dependent on grant funding it provided the continuity and financial security needed to retain successful long term programs.

The funding in 1994 also allowed the city to open fifteen alert centers throughout the city, fund thirty-five treatment beds, insured over thirty-six thousand students for treatment of substance abuse, closed one hundred forty known drug houses and the number of neighborhood associations grew from fifteen to ninety-two.

I left Alexander Youth Services after almost sixteen years in the field of juvenile justice. I am now transitioning very smoothly into community based programming working as a consultant, grants writer and programs developer for a couple of nonprofit organizations.

I eventually found the perfect program in 93' when I accepted employment and went to work for Philander Smith College's Brother-to-Brother afterschool program and as the Campus Prevention Coordinator. Under the leadership of the director Jimmy Cunningham Jr. the program was housed on the whole second floor of Liberty Hill Baptist Church and funded by a five-year federal grant plus many local funding sources. It was a sight to behold the way we furnished the center.

Purchasing hundreds of books from Pyramid Galleries we built our own library with books targeted to stimulate reading for black boys, a computer lab with a dozen stations, a recreation room with all the amenities, a physical fitness room and classrooms for group meetings. We also fed the boys nutritious snacks and a full dinner which we ate together as a family before they left for home. My job was to seek funding, promote the center and its activities, teach and be a mentor all the while coordinating Philander Smith College's campus prevention, intervention and treatment programs and teaching freshmen composition.

Dr. Myer Titus, president of Philander Smith allowed me the flexibility to continue my public volunteer work as a member of the task force but now I am representing the college's afterschool program and my role as a representative of DIGNITY is fading.

In 1995 The Martin Luther King Commission held its first Youth Assembly under the leadership of its first director Tracy Steele, a native of North Little Rock and former special assistant for economic and community development in the office for Governor Bill Clinton.

A tall, handsome young black man, Tracy was a role model and a positive face of leadership not often seen in Little Rock. Tracy, Ken, Jimmy and another young brother I also liked, Tauheed Salaam were the up and coming black men taking significant roles in the community with their work ethic, leadership, purpose and integrity.

1995 was also the year of the Million Man March. Between 800,000 and 2.2 million black men, women and people of other races came to the nation's capitol Washington D.C. and vowed to make changes back home while electrifying a shocked nation and world.

Minister Louis Farrakhan challenged black men around the nation to a Day of Atonement. Atonement is part of an eight step process including pointing out wrong, acknowledgement of wrong, confession, repentance, atonement, forgiveness, reconciliation and restoration.

The announcement of the Million Man March drew the attention of our new Youth Advisory Council President, Carlos Reece and Vice-president Changus Bell who were proactive black males and college students at Philander Smith College.

They met as a council and voted to request to make the trip to D.C. if approved by the renamed Little Rock Task Force for Youth. Their presentation to the task force was compelling and they appealed as males wanting to bond with men of influence, and to visit Howard University a noted black historical college. This would be the first educational, cultural and historic opportunity for youth. They were researching their Diaspora and for some it would be their first trip out of the state. The task force overwhelmingly voted to fund up to $5,000 for the trip after the advisory council youth presentation of the value they saw in making the journey. They spent weeks previously discussing the issues of responsibility, the role of black males and the public's perception of them. Thirty-three male students and thirteen adults boarded a bus on October 14, 1995 and traveled to Washington D.C. to attend the Million Man March, visit Howard University and tour the Capitol Mall. The bus ride to D.C. was very similar to the Spike Lee movie "*Get on the Bus*" about a group of black men taking a cross-country bus trip in order to participate in the Million Man March.

Along the way, we as men got to know each other better, discuss various topics including our personal lives, our political beliefs but without the movie's drama.

We arrived that evening in Virginia one hundred or so miles away from D.C. We spent the night at the hotel we reserved for the night because there were no rooms closer. We spent the night coordinating maps and locations to meet up if we became separated.

When we arrived on the Capitol mall it was about 3 am. Its wet cold and foggy but our spirits of being in D.C. the nation's capitol for this historic event would not be numbed by the cold. As we made our way towards the west steps of the Capitol nearly a hundred thousand people were already gathered there.

For whatever the reason (GOD) as fate would have it and it happened totally by accident DIGNITY founder Bill Walker who flew in to the march by plane and was not with the group still found us in the midst of all of these people. It was right at day break when it all started to happen. Almost magically and from the direction of the Washington Monument over a mile away there was this massive movement of people heading towards us. There were men marching and chanting something I could not quite recognize because of the distance but I knew something special was about to happen.

Almost immediately it seems as if a million people appeared from behind the surge of humanity that was still approaching the west steps of the Capitol. For the first time in my life I actually saw over a million people mainly black men come together for a Day of Atonement and reconciliation in the Million Man March.

As an Arkansas black state legislator and a politician, Bill had the ability to move about in areas not normally accessible to others. It was through this accessibility that allowed me to actually set up our viewing spot to witness the event from the Capitol Mall steps along the route in which all of the speakers were being escorted to the stage area. Both of us wearing our DIGNITY caps allowed me access to get within a few feet of famous black people from all over the world and every known walk of life. I was even able to reconnect again with Dick Gregory who recognized me. I also proudly displayed our large black DIGNITY banner that a couple of the youth held up for me. It became an instant magnet for the cameras. Thousands of men and women posed and took pictures in front of that sign. It made me feel very special knowing our banner would be seen in photos for years to come all over the country from this event.

It even drew a reporter from the Final Call, the Muslim news publication who published a quote from me about the organization in its historic news publication. The event was breathtaking and exciting. To see the many famous and noted faces, the speakers from all over the world together for such an event and to witness it was special indeed. Later that afternoon we made the planned visit to Howard University completing the trip's itinerary and purpose. These are the names of the students who attended: James Barron, Nathan Clayborn, Frank Foster, Marcus Boykin, Steven Talley, Stanley McKinney, Fred Stanton, James Allen, Kamious Butler, Harold Bush, Parnell Riley, Corey Bell, Robert Stovall, Larry Williams, Jerricho Rideout, Changus Bell, James Jordan, Marcus Burley, Roshaun Guines, Carlo Reece, Chris Ellison, Darnell Stockstill, Ivan Stevens, Tommy Payne, John Grant, Marcus Dennis, Markell Davenport and

Groesbeck Parham all acted appropriately, represented themselves well and everyone under our care returned home to Little Rock safely.

The five thousand dollar trip included a bus ride to Washington and back plus one night's stay in a hotel. A good investment in our youth you would think?

Hardly.

Upon our safe return to Little Rock we were met by news reporters with microphones and television cameras as soon as we got off the bus that Tuesday night. Seeing the many camera lights we were under the impression they were here to do stories on our adventure and journey getting positive responses from the youth of what they saw and experienced.

Wrong! What we didn't know was..............

The Little Rock Board of Directors voted nine to one that very night of our return to Little Rock to demand the city's Task Force for Youth pay back the five thousand dollars of city money spent for the trip to the Million Man March.

The board made the decision and voted after City Director Jesse Mason Jr. suggested that the task force reimburse the city. Michael Keck a city director who is now chairman of the Task Force for Youth said the money was spent appropriately and well discussed before the task force approved it. Keck was the lone no vote. Keck is white. Mason, who made the motion to seek reimbursement, is black. Once informed of the situation we decided as a group that no one from the group would make any individual statement to the press about the matter.

What we learned in D.C. we would immediately put to use. We're asked to Atone even before we "got off the bus". We met as a group the next day with virtually everyone showing up to discuss how we, not the task force would handle the demand made by the city directors of Little Rock. Utilizing what we learned at Million Man March we decided to take ownership of the debt. Only the participants who made the trip and our supporters would work collectively to collect the funds to repay the city directors.

A decision was made on how to handle the city's demand.

We marched to the steps of the nation's Capitol for a significant cause; we decided to march again to the steps of Little Rock's city hall that Wednesday to make a press announcement. The guys contacted their friends to come out and show support for us. Ken and I was the co-chair of the task force committee, we supervised the trip, but it was the leadership among these young men who stood boldly that day and announced to the city that we would indeed pay back in full every penny spent on us. To reinforce their pledge, we had a 3 by 5 foot promissory check for the five thousand dollars printed made out to the city, signed by everyone who took the trip to Washington D.C.

Of course the news reports lead story that night on television was of our press conference responding to the city director's decision to demand the money back. The immediate negative fall-out began especially from the black leadership; clergy and liberal whites called for a special meeting to reconsider their decision and to rescind their demands. Many people felt the city leaders focused more on Louis Farrakhan as leader of the Nation of Islam than for educational benefits the trip was promoting. It was a day of atonement, prayer and inspiration for black men. Across the nation critics of the march condemned the march because many were fearful to see so many blacks men come together peacefully. Something no one could envision. But one only had to watch the nationally televised event to witness that there were people of all races and thousands of women there, also

There was even one contingent I personally witnessed of one thousand black female students from Howard University who showed up and made sure it was known in their strong powerful voices that black women were there in full support of their black men.

During the press conference we announced that beginning that Friday we would hold car washes, cookie and cake bake sales, run errands and clean yards by raking leaves.

We established a special bank account where donations could be sent on behalf of the group and a contact number to request errand services.

With the story now running on the evening news and Thursday's newspapers, the outrage is growing towards the city directors especially Jesse Mason. Gloria Wilson a first-term city director also a black voted for the return of funds and though she did not speak in opposition to the trip she too felt the harsh sting of criticism deservedly so.

I never felt prouder that day as I stood in the background watching this group of young black male teenagers not associated with any gangs soon to be men showing maturity with clarity of voice and purpose with a determination to succeed beyond all doubt.

By Friday almost all of the money had been raised and over the weekend the rest was raised primarily through donations taken to the car wash sites and the bank account we established for donations. However the pressure from the community caused the directors to rescind their demand for repayment and the money collected was donated to the task force for youth special events which I believe evidentially became a future budget line item. I have special admiration for Kwami, Carlos, Changus, Sylvester, Matthew, Chris and Rochelle and the sisters Sarita and Monica. I am sure they all are still in positions of leadership even today. My story now fades away but I know that as my story ends there were many new stories that have grown from the actions of these few men of ÐIGNITY with faith in a just God to use their ÐIGNITY as its purpose to accomplish a goal to reclaim their community and share it with the world.

The reason I decided to write this story is because Little Rock's rich history is fraught with many such stories of courage and determination in the midst of turmoil and struggle.

As a community of people we have the enduring strength to persevere in the face of adversity but I also wanted to tell the world that Arkansas had ÐIGNITY a long time before Home Box Office showed up to make "Gang Banging in Little Rock".   The End

A warning to drug dealers

Johnny Hasan hands out a flier to Crystal Stewart (left) and Tavarius Smith, both 9, at a house on Gaines Street on Wednesday. DIGNITY was distributing fliers saying it has expanded its anti-drug campaign into two new areas in Little Rock. Rep. Bill Walker Jr., DIGNITY's vice president, has given drug dealers 48 hours to leave. Article on Page 4B.

In Memorarium

Million Man March 1995

In memory of our brother, Brent Woods

Post Script: Quotes, comments and specific activities were gathered through public records, publications and my memory to provide a detailed record of DIGNITY's service to our neighbors in Little Rock, Arkansas during a critical phase of its community development.